Just Passing Through

A nomadic life afloat in France

Mary-Jane Houlton

Print edition, published 2020

Copyright © Mary-Jane Houlton, 2020

This book is a memoir. It reflects the author's recollections of experiences over time. Any opinions expressed within this book are the author's personal opinions and do not reflect those of any other person or organisation.

Book cover design by ebooklaunch.com

Contents

Introduction

Less is more

There is something irresistibly romantic about the idea of living on a boat. It suggests a life of freedom, of open skies and sun on your face, a simpler yet richer existence.

In 2016, my husband Michael and I made the decision to sell our house, rid ourselves of all our possessions, close down our business and buy a motor cruiser to explore the inland waterways of Europe. We did this because we were looking for a different way of living. After decades of trying to establish roots and settle down, we finally accepted that we were nomadic by nature, forever restless, always needing to know what was around the next corner. We had also realised that the modern-day treadmill of earn-more-to-buy-more made no sense to us. We had never been materialistic but now we found we wanted even less, not more.

This book is a record of our travels, but I hope it also gives an insight into how it feels when you walk out of a secure and comfortable life and into another, very different one. We soon learnt that everything changes when you live on the water. Some days are filled with wonder, whilst others can be frustrating and challenging. On deck our horizon expanded, but inside the boat our living space contracted – there is an art to living in small spaces with few possessions. Relationships, not just with each other, but also with the friends and family we left behind, would need to be strong to survive the demands of this type of life. Some passed the test, others did not. On a personal level, when faced with so much that was unknown and which, at times, took me far out of my comfort zone, I came to know myself better. I am not sure if this life changed me, or simply brought something that had always been there, buried deep within me, to the surface.

I hope you enjoy our adventures as much as we have. Should any reader be tempted to follow in our footsteps, I have included an information section at the end of the book with practical advice to help you on your way.

PART ONE: HOW IT ALL BEGAN

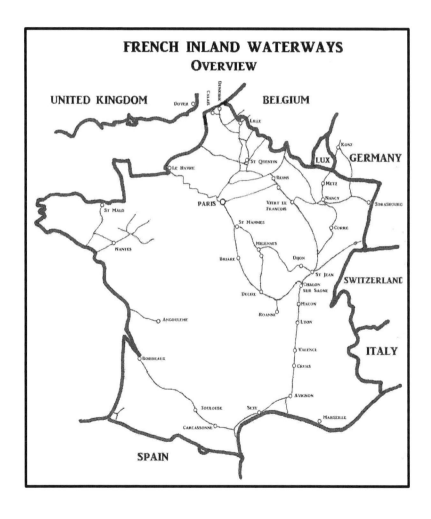

Chapter 1

Going for a song

'Do you think anyone will come?' I looked anxiously up at the sky. The clouds were that particular shade of grey that we do so well in winter in the UK, leaching the colour out of everything, and the wind was picking up.

Michael shrugged. 'We'll soon find out.'

It was the middle of January in north Wales and we were holding a yard sale. Not just any old yard sale. We'd sold our house six months ago in order to buy a boat. We'd bundled all our worldly goods into storage in our rush to get onto the water in France before the winter. That had only ever been a short-term solution, and today was the day of reckoning.

The sum total of the last fourteen years of our lives together lay sprawled around the storage container yard. The furniture from a four-bedroom cottage; a huge collection of tools we'd amassed over the years as we renovated our home and which we knew would go for a fraction of what they were worth; pictures, rugs and ornaments, curtains, garden pots and countless personal items that were worth nothing to anybody else but held years of memories for us.

Some items were harder to part with than others. Michael's

face took on the expression of a grieving relative each time he walked past his precious sea kayak. I ran sad, apologetic fingers over a book collection that went back to my childhood. It felt as if we were selling off old friends.

There is nothing that will keep the great British public from the prospect of grabbing a bargain, and so I needn't have worried about the weather. They burst in through the gates as if this was the last yard sale they would ever see, jostling for prime position and the chance to be the first to find that priceless heirloom that we might have overlooked. We were short on heirlooms, but it didn't seem to matter. They riffled through boxes, peered eagerly inside wardrobes, fingered the fabrics and fiddled with electrical goods. They haggled down, we haggled up and the pile of our possessions slowly disappeared.

Two of our friends turned up to help and surveyed the scene with a look of mounting panic on their faces.

'What can we do?' they asked, as I looked helplessly at the sea of faces in front of me and tried to remember if I'd really said it was only a fiver for my favourite wool rug.

'Pile in anywhere you like.' I nodded towards the table stacked high with the contents of the kitchen. 'That would be a good place to start.'

'Is it all priced up?'

'Nope. We tried but gave up. Too many things. Just do the best you can.'

It was a crazy day. There was no time for a cup of coffee, for lunch, even to go to the loo, let alone time to feel sad or peeved at things we had worked so hard to buy disappearing for mere pennies. If anything, there was a sense of elation as the day wore on and we realised that we were going to sell the lot.

By four pm the yard was empty save for a van from the local reclamation yard. He had offered us a deal on anything that was left. We heaved an old wardrobe up, squeezed in the last of the cardboard boxes beside it and let out a sigh of relief as it spluttered its way out of the gates. Suddenly it was quiet.

'I need a beer,' said Michael.

We took over a table in the corner of the local pub and counted up piles of notes and coins around our drinks and packets of crisps. It came to just over £2,000. We looked at each other, unsure whether to laugh or cry. It was a poor price for all the things that had made our house a home, but then I guess that much of what we'd owned had been more shabby than chic. We knew we could have got a better return if we'd sold the quality items individually over the internet but we didn't have the time, or a base from which to do it.

On the other hand, £2,000 bought us another six weeks of time on the water, which was how we now measured the value of money. We had achieved what we set out to do today, which was to rid ourselves of the last ties from our previous life.

It was done. We were free.

Chapter 2

Wanderlust

Looking back, I can't recall the exact moment when we decided to sell our house and leave the country. Momentous decisions rarely happen overnight, but there is often a catalyst, a seemingly innocent event or thought that sets the process in motion. The conversation that changed our lives is etched upon my memory, as clear to me now as if it happened only yesterday.

We were on a camping holiday in France in the summer of 2016, strolling along the Canal de Briare at Rogny-les-Sept-Écluses, admiring the barges tied up alongside the canal. A trestle table had been set up on the grassy slope beside one of the boats, a couple of stones lodged under the legs in a not entirely successful attempt to keep it level. Sanders, grinders, screwdrivers, spanners and a selection of old paint pots clung precariously to the sloping table top. Standing next to it, holding a paintbrush, was a man in overalls spattered with paint from a lifetime of DIY. As we came closer he pushed his glasses up onto his forehead and peered at us intently.

'Want to buy a boat?'

We laughed, slightly taken aback, and said we'd never thought to own a boat. The paintbrush went down on the table and out came the whole story.

'We've been all over Europe on this boat. She needs a bit of work on her, but she's sound.' He sighed. 'Never thought I'd see the day when she had to go, but my wife's got health problems and can't get about like she used to. Do you want a look around? I'll give you a good price.'

He looked so earnest that it was hard to say no, but we wished him good luck and left him to his painting. A few days later we were back home in Wales, unaware that the thought of owning a boat came with us, hidden in our subconscious and biding its time.

The views from our cottage in north Wales were spectacular, a panorama of sea and sky and mountain. I sat alone on the bench in the garden and scowled at all that open space.

'I know this is wonderful. Why does it feel like a prison?'

There was no answer.

'Why do I have all this and yet it doesn't make me happy?'

The sea, sky and mountain took no notice, too grand and lofty to care.

This inner turmoil was not new ground to me. It happened every few years. I would buy a house and try to settle down, to become part of the local community and put down roots. It never worked. Before long I would start to get itchy feet, yearn for a new challenge, new faces, new places. The house would go back on the market and I would move on yet again.

It wasn't just the string of endless house moves that was wearing me down. Since graduating with a degree in Business Studies in 1983, thirty-three years ago, I'd had sixteen different jobs. Career number one was in marketing, working for various multinational corporations. For career number two I'd tried my hand at the 'being my own boss' route to happiness, beginning with a garden design company, then a bed-and-breakfast venture, and finally a carpet cleaning business. Along the way I've also been a market trader, a kitchen designer, a Pilates instructor, a campsite health and safety inspector and a travel writer. Some of these jobs lasted for a few years, some for only a few months.

I know that for many people their jobs define them, give them an essential sense of who they are. Looking at my track record, I can only say that I know who I'm not. Maybe it all boils down to the same thing in the end.

After more than thirty years of living like this I'd got to the point where I knew I couldn't keep just moving on. It wasn't solving the problem. The part of my brain that had locked onto that conversation by the boat in France saw its chance, and an image of a tree-lined canal floated into my mind. If I'd married a man who'd trodden a conventional path through life this might have been the point where it all ended in tears. Luckily for me, Michael had also spent his life on the move, albeit in a very different way. When I found him doing an internet search on boats for sale in France I knew he was as ready for change as I was.

'Our problem is that we've got terminal wanderlust. A boat is the answer,' said Michael as he scrolled through a bewildering selection of boats. 'Whenever we get restless, we simply start the engine, throw off the ropes and off we go. Freedom. No more estate agents. No more stressful house sales.'

'We'd have to get rid of all of this stuff, this clutter,' I mused to myself, looking round the house with a critical eye. 'Life would be so much simpler.'

It got to the point where having a boat was all we could think about. Every day we found yet another reason for why it was such a good idea, but eventually common sense muscled in.

'We need to take a step back. We're getting carried away. What's the downside? What could go wrong?'

We looked at each other and waited. The silence lengthened.

'If we find we don't like it, we'll never be able to buy a house like this again,' Michael said at last, 'but I can live with that.'

'So can I. This is one of those things that we won't know is a good idea until we try it. If it doesn't work out, we'll pick ourselves up and move on. I'd rather try and fail, than spend the rest of my life regretting what might have been. Besides, I'm sure we'll love it. This feels right.'

So that was the end of that conversation. Our tiny seedling of an idea had turned into a giant, prize-winning specimen, and had become utterly irresistible. It was time, one last time, to put the house on the market and try something completely, wonderfully different.

Chapter 3

Learning the ropes

While we waited for the house to sell, we started to research how we would make this new life work. We also needed to decide what sort of boat we wanted. It took us eight months to find the right one. During that time we must have looked at hundreds of boats online and at least forty in the flesh.

Buying a boat is, in some ways, similar to buying a house. You know within minutes, almost seconds, when you've found the right one. We knew straight away that Olivia Rose was going to be the one for us. She was a Dutch-built Molenkruiser, a steel-hulled motor cruiser forty feet long and eleven feet wide, perfect for the canals and rivers of Europe, painted in a crisp two-tone combination of a royal blue hull with a white upper deck.

Having looked at many boats of all shapes and sizes, both in the UK and in Europe, she satisfied all our practical requirements but that wasn't what finally clinched the deal. She just felt right. This feeling that something is either right, or isn't, is the mantra by which we live our lives and, whilst it hasn't always worked out as we expected, we don't know how to live any other way.

Olivia had spent the last nine years moored up on the River Trent in Nottinghamshire and her owners lived aboard her. This meant that she was already kitted out as a year-round home, unusual as most boats are used for the summer months only. She had a good size walk-around bed, a proper shower and a wood burner, as well as central heating and a washing machine. Inside, both ceilings and walls were timber-clad and softly varnished. I took one look at the wooden table in the well-equipped galley and could already taste the simple suppers we would cook there, the wine glowing ruby red in the candlelight as we sat with friends old and new, sharing stories and talking late into the night.

She was built in 1991, which made her twenty-six years old when we bought her, but her present owners had taken great care of her and she was immaculate. We had the necessary surveys carried out and all seemed well. Her DAF engine, a massive beast of a thing housed beneath the floor in the wheelhouse, was older than she was. For some reason the boatbuilders had installed a reconditioned engine with twenty years on the clock into a new boat, which meant that our engine was forty-six years old. Knowing what we know now, this might have rung a few alarm bells, but hindsight has ever been a wonderful thing.

What we fervently hoped would be our last-ever house sale proved to be more stressful than all that had gone before and so we nearly lost the sale and nearly lost Olivia and everything got hopelessly delayed, but we did, finally, get through it, and so on August 3rd 2017 Olivia Rose became our new home. We had intended to sail her from Newark, round the coast and across the Channel, but it was now so late in the season that if we ran into bad weather and had to wait it out in Ramsgate there was a chance we wouldn't get over to France at all this year. Instead Olivia found herself being craned out of the water and onto the biggest trailer I've ever seen. She crossed over to France inside a P&O ferry rather than under her own steam, and on August 22nd slid gracefully down the causeway and into the water at Dunkirk.

On board were Michael and myself and our two dogs, Lucy and Maddie. Lucy is mainly Collie, fifteen years old with her eyesight, hearing and back legs not what they used to be, whilst Maddie is mainly Springer spaniel, eight years old on paper but still a puppy as far as she is concerned. Their lives until this point had been of a free-range nature in the Welsh mountains. Lucy was scared of water. Maddie loved water but was scared of everything else.

Our plan was simple. After buying Olivia we were left with a reasonable pot of money from the house sale. We had no intention of frittering away our savings but we felt comfortable in allowing ourselves two years on the water. After that, given our previous track record, we would know whether this life suited us or whether we would be moving on to something new yet again.

Europe offers rich pickings for exploration by water. We had decided to begin our journey in France because it has over 2,000 kilometres of navigable canals and rivers and is well set up for the novice boater. Heading south from Dunkirk, we had no particular destination in mind, an important feature in our new lifestyle. If we liked a place we would stop. If it didn't appeal, we would simply pass through.

Those first few weeks presented us with a steep learning curve, for me and the dogs if not so much for Michael. Neither of us had owned a boat before but Michael had spent the first nineteen years of his working life at sea, beginning as a cadet in the Royal Fleet Auxiliary. He gained his Master Mariner Certificate and, after ten years, left the RFA to work as a Navigation Officer for P&O cruise liners. These ships were as different from Olivia as it was possible to be, towering 12 storeys high, carrying 2,700 passengers and 1,400 crew. His travels had taken him around the Caribbean, the Mediterranean, the Americas and the Far East.

By the time I met him he had downsized to much smaller boats, working for Trinity House, the organisation responsible for maintaining the lighthouses and lightvessels around England and Wales. When I first asked him what he did for a living, he simply said he changed light bulbs.

For Michael, life on Olivia would require that he learnt to handle a smaller boat, and a very simple one, with no electronic navigational aids.

I knew nothing about boats. Absolutely nothing. But when was that a reason not to do anything? I would have a good teacher and hopefully our marriage would still be intact after a few weeks of him telling me what to do and when to do it.

One of the first things I had to learn was the language. Not French, in which I was reasonably fluent, but the language of boats which, to the uninitiated, can seem baffling and unnecessary. For me, learning this new language at the same time as learning how to manoeuvre Olivia into tight spaces was especially testing.

'Go astern,' Michael would say.

'What?'

'Push the throttle right back. She needs to go backwards.'

'Why can't you just say that?'

'I just did. Go astern. And if you don't do it quickly we're going to hit that wall.'

For mooring up or going into the locks there was always a decision as to whether we would tie up port side (left) or starboard side (right). The front of the boat was called the bow, and the back was the stern or simply aft. Whilst the ropes could be referred to as ropes, they were also known as lines. In the early days, on the phone to friends and family and describing our lovely new home, I would watch in fascination as Michael's eyebrows rose ever higher until they all but disappeared, as I described the kitchen (the galley) and the bedroom (the cabin). In the end, if you can't beat them you join them, and now I can do boatspeak as well as anybody.

Once I started to think about it, I realised that everyday language is peppered with nautical expressions, from three sheets to the wind to pushing the boat out, from broad in the beam to learning the ropes.

And while we're talking about learning the ropes, a surprising amount of our time was spent throwing lines around bollards in locks and alongside when we moored up for the night. Our record so far is twenty-seven locks in one day on the Canal du Nivernais and that is a goodly amount of rope throwing. We work as a team. I look after the bow end and Michael the stern.

I soon realised that ropes have a mind of their own. If they can tangle themselves into a knotty mess, they will. If they can miss the bollard by an inch, or even go on and then flip off again, they will. Bollards are also tricky things. Whenever I thought I had got the hang of it, they would change position, size or style. When mooring up in windy weather, on a fast flowing river or with a lock-keeper who is in a hurry to open the sluice gates and unleash a torrent of water into the lock, there is no time to get it wrong. You need a quick, accurate throw that goes on first time, a knot that stays knotted and tidy ropes that behave themselves instead of ending up like a pile of deranged spaghetti at your feet.

It took me a while to get the hang of this, and a reasonable amount of bad language, much to the delight of the lock-keepers, but I have now come to know my ropes. I know how high and how far I can throw, how they will behave differently when drenched and heavy with rain. They keep me physically fit and strong and, even though I must have thrown my ropes a thousand times by now, I still get a little glow inside when they loop perfectly round the bollard.

We had consciously chosen a life that was lived at a much slower pace but we hadn't fully realised what that would feel like. The speed limit on canals is eight kilometres per hour, set at that rate to minimise the erosion of the banks. To put that into a more meaningful context, it would not be unusual for us to cover a mere eighteen kilometres in a day, at an average of three kilometres an hour, passing through typically ten to fourteen locks, and perhaps a lifting road bridge that we had to operate manually ourselves. And of course that included the mandatory one-hour break for the lock-keepers to have their lunch.

If we got stuck behind a slow-moving hotel boat, or had to share locks with people in the holiday rental boats who were learning as they went – and terrifying all of us in the process – it could take even longer. Lock gates can jam or get blocked, taking all day to fix and causing a massive traffic jam of boats, who have no choice but to moor up where they can and wait it out.

This really was life in the slow lane, as far removed from eating up the miles in a car as it is possible to be. On a particularly slow day, it would be quicker to walk – but that misses the point entirely.

The dogs were also having to adapt to life on board and it soon became clear that they much preferred the space and serenity of the Welsh mountains. The first time we started up the engine they both thought the boat was being blown up and scuttled off to the nearest dark corner they could find. I almost joined them. When you're standing in the wheelhouse with the engine banging and clanging wildly beneath your feet it does have an apocalyptic edge to it.

Old age, poor eyesight and weak back legs meant that Lucy, our black and white Collie, was becoming unpredictable. Michael had the floor up in the wheelhouse one morning, checking the oil levels, with Lucy supposedly safely curled up under the galley table behind him. For some reason that only she will ever understand, she decided she wanted to be up in the wheelhouse, and launched herself in a rare burst of energy up the steps, somehow squeezing past Michael whose body was blocking her way. Unable to see that the floor was no longer there, she sailed out into thin air like something out of a Tom and Jerry cartoon and fell straight into the engine bay. Thankfully nothing was hurt except her dignity, but after that we realised we would have to keep an eye on her at all times.

Getting on and off the boat also proved tricky because her hips would often let her down just when she needed them most. Our first day in Dunkirk, whilst psyching herself up to jump from the pontoon onto the boat, her back legs gave way and she slid off backwards into the water and disappeared completely. A second later she reappeared, looking like the proverbial drowned rat, hyperventilating and thrashing about wildly, and had to be pulled out by the scruff of her neck. Once on dry land she seemed completely unconcerned, which is more than can be said for me as I thought I'd managed to drown my dog within twenty-four hours of arriving in France. I was a quivering wreck.

After that we began to lift her on and off the boat, a procedure which she detested and made as difficult as possible by wriggling with such determination to get free that we could hardly hold her. Her body may have been getting on a bit, but in her head she certainly didn't need any help from us. Which just goes to prove that dogs can delude themselves about encroaching old age just as well as humans can.

Our younger dog, Maddie, found the whole experience unsettling but then this was no different to life on land. She had always been a dog who was scared of everything and now she had a new set of terrors to overcome. On the plus side, there were more people here than in our previous home on an isolated mountain in north Wales, and she adored meeting new people. The other main joy of her life, to roll in fox poo or dead sheep carcasses, gained a new dimension *à la française* as the sheep carcasses were replaced by dead fish, which we all soon learnt had a far more pungent, and long-lasting, aroma.

PART TWO: 2017

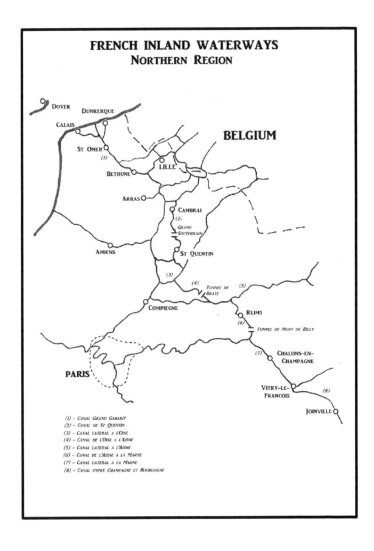

FRENCH INLAND WATERWAYS
NORTHERN REGION

(1) – CANAL GRAND GABARIT
(2) – CANAL DE ST QUENTIN
(3) – CANAL LATERAL A L'OISE
(4) – CANAL DE L'OISE A L'AISNE
(5) – CANAL LATERAL A L'AISNE
(6) – CANAL DE L'AISNE A LA MARNE
(7) – CANAL LATERAL A LA MARNE
(8) – CANAL ENTRE CHAMPAGNE ET BOURGOGNE

Chapter 4

Early days in northern France

Our first season began in late August 2017 in northern France, leaving Dunkirk via the canal of the Grand Gabarit and making our way down through an area of France known as the Pas de Calais.

Anybody who has arrived in this part of northern France, either by ferry or Eurotunnel, will have driven through here, usually at speed and with no intention of stopping, in order to get to somewhere more interesting.

We, however, were at the infatuation stage of our relationship both with Olivia and with our new life, savouring those early, heady days when everything was fresh and exciting. We could have cruised through hell and still had something good to say about it.

The French canal network was proving to be quite different to that of the UK, both in terms of scale and how it worked. Our only experience of canals back home was to walk along the towpath but we could still appreciate the difference. These ancient waterways and their locks were built in the 1800s, acting as major trade routes for commercial barges carrying coal, wood, grain, steel and all manner of commodities in their huge holds.

The tiny narrowboats that plied their trade through the canals of the UK looked like midgets in comparison. We were much bigger than a narrowboat but, when faced with an enormous commercial barge heading towards us at speed, we felt like midgets as well.

The locks were also bigger. Each of them in those early days represented their own challenges, from the huge seagoing lock out of Dunkirk harbour to the thirteen-metre deep lock which went by the name of La Fontinette.

'This is a real feat of engineering,' said Michael approvingly as we ascended past walls oozing slime.

'That's one way of describing it,' I muttered to myself. 'It feels more like a coffin to me.'

The canals in this part of France had a wild feel to them. There were long stretches with no towpaths. Without the cyclists or the walkers, and hardly any other boats, it felt surprisingly isolated. Nature had run rampant, revelling in this rare freedom, and the banks had turned into a jungle, the trees closing ranks and scrambling to reach the waterline. Branches on each side reached up and out in search of the light so that it felt as if we were cocooned in a green tunnel. On the odd occasion that a boat did appear coming towards us there was a moment of panic, as we wondered if there was enough room for two boats to pass and which of us would end up half-buried in the undergrowth. It had a distinctly Tolkienesque feel to it, with branches snagging on clothing and hair as if they were trying to pull you ashore.

Such a natural habitat was a haven for birds and their songs filled the air around us, each competing against the other, a joyous, chaotic medley that never failed to bring a smile to my face.

Sadly, we soon came to realise that there was a darker side.

Canals are man-made structures and man thinks only of himself. To ensure that the water in these big ditches does not drain away, they are edged with metal or concrete cladding, which runs either vertically, or at a very sharp angle, from up to two feet above the waterline and then straight down into the water. If an animal falls in, it can't get out.

'Please say that's not what I think it is.' I leant over the rail, peering at a sodden lump floating past us.

'What is it this time?' asked Michael quietly.

'Too far gone to tell.'

We carried on silently, the joy wiped from the day. I had never seen so many dead animals. Foxes, cats and kittens, deer and badger floating past, bloated and misshapen, some of their little bodies so distorted that we couldn't even tell what animal they had been. The deer always seemed the worst, so graceful in life and so grotesque in this horrible death. We had never experienced anything like this and it was deeply upsetting, just one more example of how mankind does what it wants and doesn't worry too much about the consequences. We personally never saw any animal fall in, we just kept coming across the end result, floating swollen and rancid in the calm waters. We assumed it always happened at night, and that they fell in by accident, but we passed a boat later on in our travels and the couple on board yelled out exultantly across the water that they had just pulled a live deer out onto the bank.

Small victories.

In other places these northern canals opened a window onto their industrial past and offered a very different, and fascinating, perspective. As we cruised along the industrial warehouse fronts in Rheims, we saw them not through our own eyes but through the eyes of the barge man bringing his *péniche* (commercial barge) alongside, loading steel or sand or grain, much as his father would have done before him. Everything here was on the grand scale, for these commercial barges are big beasts. The quays were high, with solid bollards strong enough to take the weight of a 250 tonne leviathan, considerably heavier than Olivia who weighed in at a mere 15 tonnes. Behind the towering gantries and gigantic factory doors we could see jumbo-sized reels of coiled steel waiting to be loaded aboard. It was as if the world had suddenly scaled up to a land of giants.

As a motorist or a casual sightseer you would have no way of knowing that this world even existed. We cruised slowly by, peering unashamedly into factory after factory. Most of them were empty, eerily silent. The quayside stretched on forever, long enough to take a whole fleet of barges, but here there was only one. Just one solitary barge moored up in all that empty space, and it was being loaded with sand, a fountain of golden grains spurting out of a long tube before being swallowed within the cavernous depths of the boat's hold.

These hauliers of the canals have been replaced by truckers of the road. The growth of rail freight has also struck a mortal blow, and now there are just a few isolated commercial barges still plying their trade. We were looking at a way of life in its death throes.

Cruising on past, we soon found ourselves closer to the city centre. At one point the canal ran parallel with the main road, so close that we could smell the exhaust fumes and see the faces of people in their cars, driving on autopilot to another day at work. For a moment I had a flashback as to how my life used to be, staring unseeingly ahead as I too slogged my way to work every morning. For a few minutes it was as if time had temporarily warped, my old life and my new running side by side, as we chugged along at eight kilometres per hour while the cars sped past us, their passengers unaware, locked inside their own worlds.

Further down, on the Canal de St Quentin, we cycled into the city of St Quentin for food supplies. The weather had turned against us, smothering the town in a persistent, miserable drizzle. If the main square had anything special about it, no-one was taking any notice, hunched up and hurrying to get out of the rain.

Lunch was a soggy affair, sheltering under an archway and eating a disappointing baguette. Sharing our precious dry space were the teenagers let loose on their school lunch break, some of them paired off and busy exploring the food of love rather than anything of a culinary nature.

'I'm sure I didn't spend all my lunch hour snogging when I was that age.' I was trying hard not to stare at one particular couple who were so entwined it was hard to work out where he ended and she began.

'Looks like he's eating her, rather than kissing her. Enough to put you off your lunch.' Michael took a last bite of his baguette and grimaced. 'Which wouldn't be difficult.'

Some of the moorings were also industrial in nature and very different to the idyllic image of a rural and beautiful mooring spot that I had always pictured in my daydreams.

We usually managed to avoid these but, after one very long day when our first choice for the night was full and the second was inexplicably chained off, we found ourselves with no other option.

'You have got to be kidding,' I said. 'There's no way we're stopping here.'

Our potential berth for the night was directly opposite a commercial coal yard. Mountains of slag, like ebony pyramids, faced the mooring spot. Above them, conveyor belts screeched and squawked their way round on an endless loop, dumping the spoil on top of the closest pyramid. I could smell the coal dust in the air, feel it working its way into my lungs, sharply metallic and promising all sorts of carcinogenic repercussions. A fleet of lorries were queued by another conveyor belt system, waiting to load the coal, their throaty engines rumbling below the high-pitched whine of the belts, and then shooting up the decibel scale as they accelerated up the slope and out of the yard.

'No. We definitely can't stay here,' I said more firmly.

'I don't think we've got much choice. There's nowhere else for miles. And it's getting dark.'

So we stopped, consoling ourselves with the thought that it would all shut down for the night soon.

As dusk fell, a series of floodlights clicked on, banks of them that put me in mind of a football stadium, towering over the whole depot. The night and the longed-for silence was banished. This was a twenty-four-hour operation and so the conveyor belts kept churning out their black nuggets and the lorries kept taking it away. It was a warm September night but we had to batten down the hatches, sealing doors and windows in an unsuccessful attempt to keep the noise and dust out. The lights were so strong that they shone through our blinds as if they weren't there, casting stripes over the bed. Sleep was impossible.

In the end I gave up even trying. I got out of bed and sat up on deck, watching the lorries driving off in a flurry of coal dust and cursing them under my breath. The mountain of coal nearest to us was, for some inexplicable reason, a favoured perch for a flock of seagulls. Their feathers contrasted starkly against the inky blackness, the purest, softest shade of white. They were motionless and silent for so long that it seemed as if they weren't real and that I was looking at an artist's abstract impression of white on black.

It was a surreal snapshot, not beautiful exactly, but very striking, and for a moment my frustration with our surroundings faded away.

Thankfully most of our moorings were much better than this, quiet rural spots with the *boulangerie* a short walk away, or charming marinas with a waterside bar and convivial company to spend the evening with. But the image that remains the strongest is that of the seagulls perched on a slag heap.

No matter what happened around us, Olivia was our constant. When every single thing in your day, every day, is a new experience in a strange place, it is exciting but also challenging. She was our safe haven, familiar and reassuring.

I learnt to gauge if things were right in her world by the sounds she made, the flow of the water past her bow, the creak of the ropes and fenders at night. The most important song in her repertoire was the engine. It had a distinctive rhythm to it, whether idling or running, and both Michael and I were getting the niggling feeling that something didn't sound quite as it should. It was a smelly engine, but then it was old and a DAF and they were renowned for it. We kept a close check on the oil and water and everything was as it should be and so, as long as she kept on starting, we kept on going.

It wasn't just the sound of her, it was the feel of her too. One of my favourite places to sit as we cruised was on the deck at the bow end, my back comfortably wedged against the sloping galley windows and my feet stretched out in front of me. If we were being picky about terminology this part of the boat could also be called the fo'c'sle – the abbreviated term for the forecastle – but I'll just stick to calling it the deck.

It became part of my daily ritual to have my mid-morning

cup of tea sitting there, cradling my mug in my hands and running my eyes over the tapestry of trees and water, following the desultory flight of a heron as we disturbed it from a fishing perch. The steel deck would warm gently in the sunshine so it was like sitting on an electric blanket and I could faintly feel the thrum of the engine running through the hull, as if her heart was beating softly beneath me. Later on, when we would leave Olivia for the winter season, it was always this memory I kept close until we could be with her again for the following year.

As autumn drew in, the soft September sunshine was balanced by colder nights. Sitting by the wood burner, and without a television to distract us, we found time to talk, to play games, or simply to sit in companionable silence, watching the flames dance behind the glass. Life had slowed down – not just when we were travelling, but also when we were stationary, moored up for the night. To begin with I found it hard to relax like this. I'd always been so busy; sitting down wasn't something I ever did. I realised after a few weeks that I was going to have to re-educate myself, to learn how to use all this free time we now had.

Chapter 5

New faces

We shared the canals with a host of other users: pleasure boaters like ourselves, commercial barges and hotel boats who relied on the water for their living, as well as those who enjoyed the water from the towpath, the fishermen, walkers and cyclists. Most of these groups got along together very well.

Apart from the fishermen.

Fishing is a national obsession in France, popular with all ages, and with women as well as men. However, boaters and fishermen don't necessarily view the world in the same way.

If you go back to our hunter-gatherer days, fishing makes perfect sense. You catch a fish and you eat it. But modern-day fishing doesn't seem to work that way. It is hard to see what the attraction is in sitting glumly by the water for hours on end, never catching anything at all. On the rare occasion that an unlucky fish actually takes the bait, it is measured with a tool designed specifically for the job, photographed from all angles, and then put back in the water, where it probably quietly dies from the stress of it all.

In tune with our modern society of doing everything to excess, French fishermen don't just have one rod out in the water, they will have six or seven. Once the lures have been thrown out right into the middle of the canal, hence making it impossible for a boat to go past without running aground on the opposite bank, the fisherman will either settle down for a siesta and fall sound asleep, or abandon his lines entirely to go and relieve himself in the woods in time-honoured French fashion. When you politely ask him to either wake up or zip up, the response is rarely a gracious one. It got to the point that whenever we saw a set of lines in the water we braced ourselves.

'We've got trouble ahead.' I squinted into the late evening sun, trying to make out exactly what I was looking at. 'I think I see fishing lines.'

As we drew closer I could see that it was indeed fishing lines, five rods spaced out to fill the gap between two boats already moored up for the night. A car was parked nearby, a man reaching into the boot. He straightened up, a landing net and a bucket in his hands, and turned towards his lines. Then he saw us. The response was unmistakeable. He drew himself up, squared back his shoulders and glared.

'This is going to go well,' I muttered. 'I was hoping we could moor there.'

'Is there any space further ahead?' asked Michael.

'Hard to see. There might be something right at the end.'

'We'll go and have a look.'

We chugged past and I gave him a cheery wave on principle, which earned me a scowl, but there were no other spaces. Michael and I looked at each other.

'Ready to do battle?'

I ran through a quick mental check of the French vocabulary I would need for this encounter and nodded. We turned Olivia round and headed back to the fisherman.

This wasn't the first time this had happened. There are set places on the canals that are moorings for boats, places where we know we will have sufficient depth of water to get alongside. A fisherman is free to set his chair at any point along the towpath, but there are always a few who feel that they have the right to set up in moorings, despite signs from the relevant local authority telling them that it is forbidden to fish there and, in some cases, even despite the moorings being gated off.

In the short time it took us to get back, our fishing friend had wedged himself firmly into a rickety canvas chair with the determined air of a man who is in his rightful place and has no intention of moving.

'*Bonsoir Monsieur*,' I smiled. 'I am so sorry but you are taking a space that is reserved for boats.'

'There are spaces further on.' He stuck his chin out. 'You don't need to come in here.'

'I'm afraid we do. There are no spaces further up and nowhere else for us to moor. I am sorry to inconvenience you but we have to come in here.'

'But all my stuff.' He gestured at his rods, his buckets, his nets. 'I have taken hours to set this all out. It's not right. You can't come here.'

'There are lots of other spaces for fishing.' I pointed to the other bank. 'This space is for boats.'

'And how am I supposed to get my car over there?' He shoved himself out of his chair and pointed an accusing finger. 'You boats think you own the waterways.'

'Not at all, *Monsieur*. We are very happy to share, but we are allowed to tie up here.' I paused and said my next words very slowly, in the hope they might sink in. 'We are allowed to tie up here because this mooring is for boats. Not for fishing.'

By now we had attracted an audience. The boat moored up closest to the fishing lines was French, with a husband and wife aboard. The man came to the bow and said something to the fisherman. We couldn't hear it, but it didn't go down well, leading to more gesticulating and raised voices. The man on the boat raised his hands and shrugged apologetically in our direction. The fisherman seemed to think the matter was settled, sat back down in his chair and busied himself with baiting a line.

'Now what?' said Michael.

'We wait him out,' I said. 'We sit here, as close as you can get without snaring his lines, and we keep the engine running. He'll never catch anything with us so close and we'll see who gives up first.'

I leant over the rail.

'*Pas de problème, Monsieur*. We will just wait here until you have finished your fishing.'

'*Ah, mais non!* You can't do that. You will disturb the fish. This is very bad, very bad.'

I gave the best French shrug I could muster and went down below. Ten minutes later I was back up on deck with two mugs of tea and cake. I sat down in a chair, put my feet up comfortably on the hand rail, and sniffed the air. 'That engine is stinking a bit this afternoon.'

I don't know if it was the sight of our tea or the engine fumes wafting his way, but half an hour later he'd had enough. Rods, buckets and nets were dumped in the boot of his car and he roared off.

It would be unfair to say that all fishermen are like this, but speak to any boater and they will tell you a similar tale. As a final note on the subject of fishing, and in the spirit of do as you would be done by, we did our best to share the waterways in a considerate fashion, but I think that the one thing that would make a fishermen's day shine, apart from actually catching something, would be a canal devoid of boats.

In contrast, walkers and cyclists seemed delighted to see us and were generally much friendlier. I've lost count of the times we were wished a cheery *'Bon appétit!'* as we sat on deck enjoying lunch whilst they walked or cycled past. We got so used to this that we forgot there was any other way to behave until we came back to the UK for a short visit to see friends and family.

Taking a picnic out to a local beauty spot, we sat out on the grass not far from the footpath. In France there would have been some response from almost everybody who passed us by but here, in our own country, no-one even looked at us, let alone spoke to us. The picnic became a rather joyless occasion and I found myself longing to get back onto French soil.

There is one final group of people we came to know who cannot be left out for they make life on the water possible for all of us. These are the *éclusiers* or lock-keepers and without them the system would very quickly grind to a halt. The French canal network differs from the UK in that it is not the boat owner's responsibility to manually operate the locks. Some canals are now fully automated, but the remainder are run by the *éclusiers*, both male and female, young and old, and, whilst they will welcome your help at times, you are not allowed to operate the locks without them.

Each lock has a cottage adjacent to it and in the old days it would have been the home of the *éclusier* and his family, a base from which to manage the locks, maintain the water levels and deal with blockages and gate failures. I like to imagine it would have been a good life while it lasted.

Like so many of the old ways, that life is slowly dying out. The VNF (Voie Navigables de France) is the body responsible for running the canals and they are fighting a losing battle against falling revenues and ever-rising costs. Commercial trade has declined dramatically, budgets have been slashed and now the majority of these cottages lie empty, their windows boarded up and their roofs falling in. Each lock-keeper has to manage a string of locks, rather than just one, and it is a common sight to see them roaring up the towpath on their moped, helmet perched loosely atop their head and the straps flying in the wind, racing back and forth between boats. In the low season, when the holiday rental boats are all back in their marinas and the waterways become quieter, they are happy to chat and many have the same tale to tell.

'It is we who are paying the price,' said one. 'They cut down our numbers and expect us to do more work for less pay. We can't do our jobs properly and it is very stressful. Before long we will all be gone. The canals will be completely automated.'

His words filled me with regret. We had already passed through some canals that had been automated and it was a very different experience. At the beginning of each of these canals, boats are issued with a *télécommande*, a remote control device about the size of a mobile phone. When you come in range of a sensor on the bank, you press a button on the device and the lock's gates will open. Once inside you pull a cord to either empty or fill the lock and the gates at the other end open automatically.

There is no human contact, no chat, no smile and the journey feels somehow emptier. It is human nature to push relentlessly on, finding supposedly cheaper, ever more efficient ways of doing things. You can't help but wonder at times if we lose more than we gain.

I had heard that, whilst the French are very sociable and happy to pass the time of day, they take longer to open up and talk about things that are personal and matter to them. The more time I spent in the country, the less I found this to be the case.

'*Vous aimez le whisky?*' an older gentleman lock-keeper asked me whilst we waited for the lock to fill on a blustery autumn day.

'*Pas vraiment. Je préfère le cidre,*' I replied.

'But surely you like Scotland?'

'Oh yes. It's one of our favourite places.'

'*Moi aussi. J'adore l'Écosse.* I was going to take my wife there. To introduce her to the whisky.' He looked down and rubbed capable, calloused hands together. 'She died last year. Today is the anniversary of her death and I am sad.'

I didn't know what to say. My French wasn't up to fluent condolences, but it would have been almost as difficult to find the words in English.

'I won't go to Scotland again,' he said. 'It wouldn't be right.'

'*Je suis désolée, Monsieur,*' I said and squeezed his arm gently. The lock filled and he moved off to shut the door to the small hut where the lock controls were housed. I turned to wave as we left but he had already gone.

Chapter 6

Facing fear

'This is going to be fun,' said Michael. 'I'm looking forward to doing this.'

I wasn't. I was dreading it.

We were moored up at the northern entrance to the Riqueval Tunnel on the Canal de St Quentin. The entrance was tiny, a black, gaping maw grinning maliciously at the bottom of the hillside. We were completely alone. No boats, no people. No buildings or sheds for the staff working the tunnel, just one sign instructing us to moor up here and wait for the tug. There were no contact numbers and no times of departure.

It was a grey and gloomy day and the approach to the tunnel was through a steeply sided gorge. What little light remained would soon be gone, snuffed out. When night fell here it would be so black you wouldn't see your hand in front of your face.

I'm not exactly claustrophobic but I don't like being in confined spaces. I wasn't sure yet whether being on a boat in a tunnel was going to make that particular confined space worse or better. This tunnel, at just over five kilometres in length, is the longest canal tunnel in France, and had been the longest in the world until Italy broke the record when they built the Biassa

Tunnel in La Spezia.

It is also very old, built between 1801 and 1810 on the orders of Napoleon, using hundreds of prisoners of war as slave labourers. There is often a human price to pay for the construction of incredible structures such as this and so a number of those men died in the process. I gazed into the blackness and wondered what had happened to their bodies. This was the sort of place, if you were that way inclined, where you could believe in restless, tortured spirits. I craned my neck to look up to the top of the hill. All that rock and earth resting on a man-made structure that was over 200 years old. One of these days it was going to cave in.

I gave myself a mental shake. 'Don't be ridiculous. It'll be fine.'

'This is fascinating.' Michael was leafing through one of our many books on canals. 'When this canal was in its prime there could have been as many as thirty commercial barges going through in convoy. All pulled by just one tug. Apparently if you were at the end of the line, the boats would swing about all over the place. It says here that you can see all the scrape marks on the walls as you go through.'

'Marvellous,' I said. 'Two hundred years old and it's been bashed to bits. Definitely ripe and ready for a cave-in.'

Michael looked at me over the top of the book. 'Don't worry about it. You'll be fine.'

That was easy for him to say. He wasn't inside my head.

The Riqueval Tunnel, also known as Le Grand Souterrain, which loosely translates as The Big Underground, has no ventilation along its entire length. The fumes from the engines of thirty barges would be fatal, hence the introduction of an electric tug. All boats turn off their engines, rope up one behind the other, and are pulled through behind the tug. These days the traffic is far less; a combination of maybe five or six barges and pleasure cruisers would be more typical. I had made the mistake of researching this on the pleasure boat forums and had read horror stories about boats which had spent the journey ricocheting wildly from side to side, out of control and getting badly damaged.

As if that weren't enough, as each boat reaches the end of the tunnel it is expected to release the lines of the boat behind it, turn its engines back on and depart. The logic of this defeated me because if those lines were thrown off too soon the boat left in the tunnel would just grind slowly to a halt, and indeed I had heard of exactly that happening.

All I wanted was to get it over with, but the French laissez-faire attitude to timetables wasn't helping. There were two crossings each day but there seemed to be no clear consensus on what times they would be. We had arrived for the lunchtime crossing, but nothing appeared. There was the possibility of another one later in the evening. No-one appeared for that either. In the end we went to bed, reasoning that a tug would appear at some point the next day.

It showed up at nine am the next morning, quite outside of any of the scheduled times, crawling out of the tunnel entrance like a little white beetle, with just two boats behind it. Within minutes it had turned the boats loose, and the two guys operating it had taken our ropes and tied them to the back of the tug with nothing more than a grunt and a nod. We were off.

The tunnel was illuminated but only poorly, the fluorescent tubes above our heads pushing the darkness back just enough for us to make out the contours of the tunnel for a few metres in front of us. We had just over a metre leeway either side of the boat, with a bit more above our heads. Looking longingly back, the tunnel opening was a tiny circle of light, shrinking ever smaller until it was no more than a pinprick and then it disappeared altogether. The crossing would take two hours.

With no engine noise it was eerily quiet inside, the only sound the intermittent trickle and drip of water forcing its way out of weak spots in the rough stone. Sometimes tiny droplets landed feather-light on a cheek, other times a miniature waterfall would surprise us, always managing to find the back of our necks, running icy cold against our skin.

As I became more accustomed to the darkness I relaxed a little and started to take more notice of the details around me. On one side of the tunnel there was a narrow walkway, a subterranean towpath, which in earlier days would have been used first by the men who pulled the barges through and then the horses. Now it was used for maintenance or as somewhere to get off in an emergency. On the other side, the rough stone of the wall had been polished smooth by larger barges rubbing along it as they squeezed through. The water was inky black, and my eyes were constantly straining to find the line where the water ended and the walls began. In the half light, our shadows were projected behind us, slightly blurry around the edges, a pair of ghosts peering over our shoulders.

I was watching the distance markers etched on the walls, counting them every hundred metres and, when we finally reached the halfway mark, I could sense the tension in my shoulders easing off a little. Little by little, the pinprick of daylight that was our exit got bigger and bigger and then suddenly we were out, a wide and high sky soaring above us, the light so sharp it hurt our eyes.

The southern end of the tunnel was obviously where the organisation was based. There were buildings, people, boats waiting to go in. It felt like a different world to the northern side.

I learnt a valuable life lesson from Le Grand Souterrain. The things that you think you are afraid of will often turn out much better than you feared. We had been lucky in our crossing, for we were just one boat and not in a convoy, but even so I knew I would feel more comfortable now with any future tunnels. It is human nature to be scared of the mere thought of something, our imaginations building it up to a level that reality cannot match. The things in life that are truly terrifying, be it emotionally or physically, tend to come out of the blue, unlooked for and unexpected, and in that split second of them happening adrenalin will take over and we will just do the best we can at the time.

Whichever way it goes, I have come to the conclusion that worrying about things is a waste of my time. And in this amazing new life that we have found, I don't want to waste even a minute stressing about how I might or might not cope, or what might or might never happen at some unknown point in the future.

There is great comfort in this realisation – as long as I remember to put it into practice next time something daunting comes along.

Chapter 7

If it can go wrong, it probably will

By early October we had reached the Champagne region of France and the countryside around us changed again, the wild and tangled undergrowth replaced by neat, orderly rows of vines. The town of Châlons-en-Champagne treated us to a fine autumn display as we cruised through a tree-lined park, the leaves a glorious kaleidoscope of red, amber and gold. The lofty towers of the Cathédrale St Étienne were bathed in warm sunlight and, although we were right in the heart of the city, it was peaceful. The only discordant note was from a car alarm, wailing persistently in the background.

As we motored on, the buildings faded into the distance behind us and yet the sound of the car alarm remained constant. We looked at each other.

'Where's that coming from?'

'I don't know,' said Michael. 'Can you open the door to the wheelhouse?'

I did so and the noise suddenly got much louder.

Michael, who was in his usual driving position on top deck, leapt down the stairs and into the wheelhouse. He punched the engine cut-out button and we stood there in the now ominous silence as Olivia freewheeled gently on.

'What *was* that?'

'It's the fire alarm in the engine bay,' said Michael grimly.

I looked at the solid, heavy trap doors that made up most of the floor under our feet and beneath which resided our engine.

'What do we do now?'

'We have a think about it,' said Michael with a reasonable semblance of calm. He glanced up and down the canal. 'There's nothing coming. We can drift for a bit.'

'Are we on fire?' An image of a raging inferno beneath our feet flashed through my mind.

'I don't think so.'

'You don't *think* so? Can't you be a bit more definite than that?'

'I'm not an engineer. My job was to drive boats, not fix them.' He scratched his head.

'If we're not on fire, why did the alarm go off?'

'Because it got too hot down there. It could be the impeller. I can't smell anything burning so we'll open up the hatch.'

'Is that a good idea?'

'We'll do it carefully. Slowly.'

We eased the hatch up, inch by inch. No flames. Just the distinctive smell of a very hot engine.

'Right.' Michael sounded more like his usual decisive self and I felt the knot of unease in my stomach loosen a little. 'We'll tie up somewhere and then I'll go down and have a closer look.'

We went back up on deck, searching the banks for a suitable spot. We were lucky. A hundred yards back along the canal there were two bollards, hardly visible in the undergrowth. It was unclear as to why they were there at all, as there was no footpath in this section, but at some point back in time there would have been a reason to have a mooring here.

'Great,' I said. 'I'll turn the engine on and we'll reverse back.'

'Can't do that. Not until I know exactly what's happened. One of us needs to jump ashore and pull us back.'

I looked more closely at the bank. It was an unfriendly combination of weeds, nettles and brambles, knee high, sloping steeply down towards the water's edge. More to the point, it was a long way away.

'I don't think even you can jump that distance,' I said dubiously.

'I'm not going to. You are.'

'Why me? You always do the intrepid stuff.'

'Because I'm the skipper and a skipper always stays with his boat.'

'And I'm your wife and if you want it to stay that way, you'll think again.' I looked at the soupy brown water in horror. 'I'll never make that distance. I'll fall in and drown.'

'Now you're being melodramatic. It's probably not even six foot of water here.'

'Six foot of water and two foot of mud. I'm not doing it.'

'If you've got another suggestion I'm all ears. But we can't stay here and it's better to move soon before a commercial barge comes along and throws us all over the place.'

'Maybe someone will pass by and we can throw them a line.' I looked hopefully along the banks but they remained steadfastly empty. 'Someone walking their dog. Or even a fisherman.'

'I can go ashore if you like but if we have to get out of the way quickly that means you'll have to start the engine and deal with whatever happens. And get her alongside quick-sharpish.' Michael paused, just to make sure his next words had the desired effect. 'By yourself.'

I sighed. My driving skills were coming along but I wasn't very confident yet. The thought of being alone on the boat in this situation wasn't appealing.

'You can do it,' said Michael in the tone of someone who knows he has just won the argument. 'Imagine you're a gazelle.'

'I'm not a bloody gazelle.' I glared at him crossly.

'You are to me.'

This was accompanied by a winning smile. Needless to say, he didn't get one back.

I took a deep breath and leapt.

And landed in a tangled heap on all fours with my bottom up in the air. My feet were only just on the slope of the bank and I could feel them sliding back down so the whole graceless manoeuvre was completed by a panicky scramble up onto flat ground.

'That's my girl. I knew you could do it.' Michael threw me a line and I pulled us back the hundred yards to the bollards. Olivia weighs fifteen tonnes but it is surprisingly easy for one person to pull her along, providing there is no wind or current to fight against. In a few minutes we were moored alongside and Michael had the hatches up and had disappeared inside the engine bay.

It turned out that our impeller, which is an integral part of our engine cooling system, was shredded. This is not an uncommon problem, as we later learnt from other boaters, but we would need to fit a new one before we went on.

We didn't have another one and this was one of our first lessons in how important it is to have a comprehensive range of spares on board. As far as boats are concerned, if it can go wrong it probably will and so having spare parts is vital.

Like so many older vessels, Olivia had been tinkered about with by her previous successive owners and so we had a hotchpotch of different cooling systems. Today it worked to our benefit as it allowed Michael to bypass the impeller-cooled system for long enough to drive us back to the marina in Châlons-en-Champagne. We ordered a box of replacements over the internet and, with impressive efficiency, they arrived within twenty-four hours and we were ready to set off once more.

Unfortunately we didn't get very far. That niggling premonition that the engine wasn't entirely happy had been at the back of our minds for some days. Now it turned into a certainty.

In a bid to find a positive side to a bad situation there's nothing like a spot of engine trouble for widening your French vocabulary. If you want to chat about fuel injectors not behaving as they should, or diesel spewing out in our exhaust (where it shouldn't be), or diesel in the oil sump (which is an even worse place for it to be), or oil levels mysteriously rising when they should be stable, not to mention the fact that our ancient engine was belching out enough smoke to pollute half of France, then I'm your girl. Within a few weeks all these technical terms rolled off my tongue as if I'd spent my working life with my head buried in an engine. Even more amazingly, I almost understood how it all worked. I normally jump at any chance to improve my vocabulary but these are words I'd rather not have had to learn, for the consequences of these problems would rank this particular French lesson as the world's most expensive ever.

The problems didn't all arrive at once. Rather, they built up slowly and inexorably to a point where big decisions had to be made. An increasing number of our days were spent listening for how the engine sounded, constantly monitoring levels of water, fuel and oil, and it took all the joy out of the trip. The engine really is the heart of the boat and you have to have faith in it or there is no peace of mind. There is no RAC or AA for boat breakdowns. You're on your own and with no guarantee of a mooring spot while you try and sort it out. Before we had a boat I assumed that you could tie up anywhere, but the water is often so shallow at the edge of the canal that in many places there would be no chance of you getting in close enough to get a mooring line out.

We spoke to all and sundry about what the problem might be. All and sundry proffered up a variety of different possible causes and remedies. We found ourselves a good local mechanic from a nearby garage. This may sound an odd choice but most boat engines are lorry or tractor engines that have been 'marinised', a term that may have a culinary ring to it but actually means that they are modified for marine use.

In no time at all we had spent over a thousand euros – labour and parts cost a fortune in France – and all we had to show for it was that we were beginning to eliminate the things that weren't causing the problem without getting any closer to being certain what *was* causing the problem. As the list got slowly whittled down, it was becoming uncomfortably clear that what was left was more serious and would be even more expensive to fix.

We got to the point where we didn't know what to do for the best. We decided to stop, financially and also physically, and take a step back from it all. We halted in a little town in the middle of nowhere called Joinville, on the Canal entre Champagne et Bourgogne, in a tiny mooring offered by a hotel, tied up at the end of their garden. It was quiet and peaceful and just what we needed. We spent hours sitting up on deck, watching the autumn leaves carpeting the canal in red and gold, and talked through our options.

Part of the problem was that there was no cut and dried right or wrong decision. We were not hugely knowledgeable about engines and so had to make a judgement call based on what little information we had been able to glean and what felt right. We could keep throwing good money after bad, lurching from one costly repair to another, or we could consider a new engine.

Finally, after much soul searching, we went for the new engine.

Choosing the right engine, the right installer and the right price turned out to be a daunting, time-consuming research job. The French either weren't interested or wouldn't give a fixed price. The Dutch had a good reputation, were very efficient and upfront about costs but we would either have to undertake a long trip to get Olivia to them or they could come to us, which had further cost implications. In the end we chose an English company, highly recommended, who would come out to us and do it for what seemed a fair price.

By the end of October all decisions had been made, dates confirmed and deposits paid so we left Joinville, which after almost a month felt like home, and headed back to Châlons-en-Champagne, which had a suitable quay to allow the work to be carried out. It would take us four days to get there, time enough to prepare ourselves for the onslaught.

It would be a mammoth job. Obviously the old engine would come out first, but it was huge and incredibly heavy. At one point they thought the only way they would get it out would be to cut off the entire roof of the wheelhouse (in non-boat language this is our sitting room), which nearly brought me to tears, but in the end they got it out by stripping it down to the bare minimum in situ and then it would just, by no more than a millimetre or two, squeeze through the doors.

Because it was so heavy, they would have to build a scaffolding tower inside the wheelhouse to winch it out and then have another ratchet winch on the quayside ready to pull it up a specially constructed ramp into their van. The whole process would be repeated in reverse to get the new engine in. We, and the dogs, would still be living on board whilst all this was going on.

They allowed a two-man team five days to do the complete job, two days to get the engine out and a further three days to get the new one in and all the supporting systems reconnected. In the end it took eight days, even though they worked long hard hours, and when it was over we were all exhausted.

Having this engine put in was one of the hardest decisions we have ever had to make, much harder than deciding to sell the house and take a leap into the unknown. A mammoth job commands a mammoth price tag, in this case half the purchase price of the boat, and never in our worst nightmare had we ever imagined that we would be depleting our funds to this extent after only a few months on the water. It hurt and it took a while to get over it.

But life always goes on and so, whilst making endless cups of tea and coffee for our hard-working engineers as they grunted and sweated and carried out major heart surgery on Olivia, we used the time to work out what lay ahead for us in this first winter.

We wanted to stay on the boat but we wouldn't be cruising. The vast majority of the mooring spots in France have the water turned off in winter, to prevent burst pipes in cold weather. Often the electricity is turned off too, which means you need to pick a spot where the services stay connected. We decided to stay where we were. Châlons seemed a nice town, and the marina was situated on the edge of a beautiful park. We brought our van back over from storage in the UK so we could explore the area over the winter.

We were still very much in northern France, just over 300 miles from Calais. If you drew a straight line east from Paris we would be just above it. This meant that the weather was similar to the UK and we were slightly concerned about how we would manage the short days and long dark evenings in a country where we knew no-one. We'd never been any good at just sitting around all day either so we would have to find a way of keeping ourselves occupied. Help came from an unexpected source.

'We've got company.' Returning from walking the dogs,

Michael put their leads back on their hooks and started to divest himself of a thick coat and various under-layers. 'Coming for tea this afternoon.'

I looked at him, completely bemused.

'I met two ladies. Or rather, Maddie did. She was running back home as *les chasseurs* are out hunting today, guns banging away for all they're worth, and she hid behind two ladies, so we started talking. They like boats and they'd like to come round for tea. Three o'clock this afternoon.'

And so we were befriended by Lise, a retired French schoolteacher, and her friend Ulrike, a German lady who had married a Frenchman and had lived here all her married life.

They both spoke fluent English and were keen to practise it. We talked about their families, about when and where they had been in the UK, about Macron and how he was a president for the rich, not the poor. They belonged to a twinning association and invited us to their meetings so that the members could also practise their English.

We, of course, wanted to speak more French. Lise found us a French class being taught by a German lady to some young Armenian refugees. A more bizarre combination I couldn't imagine but it sort of worked. It was a beginners class, which was helpful for Michael although not so much for me, but as it had to go through an Armenian translator it was a slow process.

Michael spent many of the evenings teaching himself French grammar and vocabulary whilst I had subscribed to a distance learning novel writing course to help me write a novel I'd had in mind for a while. I had eight assignments to send in, from which I would get feedback, and it suited me as I needed some structure to motivate myself.

'They have no number for eighty. Instead they do four times twenty.' Michael would regularly slam his grammar book down on the table in frustration. 'Why do they make it so complicated?'

I would regularly ignore him as I was in the flow and you never interrupt a budding bestselling author when she is in the flow. He knows this, but doesn't always remember that he knows this.

As I would invariably be at a critical point in my story line, too critical to interrupt it even to say 'Shut up, I'm writing', I would keep my head down and hope he'd move on to the next conundrum without my input. It rarely worked.

We became avid birdwatchers. It was hard not to, for they were all around us. A resident kingfisher, or *martin-pêcheur* to give him his French name, used our boat rails as one of his favourite hunting perches.

We called him Martin. Why wouldn't you?

I could look out of the window and watch a cormorant, so drab compared to Martin but somehow endearing in its scruffy ugliness, swallowing a fish just three feet away from me. The swans also provided us with endless entertainment. The main group seemed to exist quite peacefully together but there were two other swans who caused mayhem whenever they got too close. We were never sure if they were last year's male offspring who were now seen as a threat, or complete newcomers, but they were regularly seen off by the dominant male. He would puff himself up to twice his normal size, bend that graceful neck into the shape of a shepherd's crook, and paddle furiously towards the intruders, murderous intent in his glassy eyes. It was a matter of pride that the outsiders left it to the last possible moment before taking flight, their powerful wings thrusting and thrumming through the air, feet hanging down like the undercarriage of a plane, and sounding strangely like a herd of wild horses taking flight.

We explored the area, went out for lots of walks, and kept an eye out for any local events that looked interesting. The best of these was an open day at a nearby champagne house. We naively assumed an open day meant it was open all day and so turned up at half past one, but of course open days are only open either side of a two-hour lunch break.

There were no other cars in the car park when we arrived, which should have given us a clue, but we went in anyway. To their credit that last thirty minutes of lunch was forsaken and we were treated to a personalised tour and tasting which introduced us to a drink we had never heard of before.

Ratafia is a fortified wine made through a distilling of the champagne grape and it gets its name due to the fact that in the days when treaties were signed, or ratified, this drink was served as a celebration. It tasted more like a liqueur than a wine and I don't normally like liqueurs but this was something else. This was heaven.

Despite the soothing effects of a glass of ratafia on those long, dark nights it was a hard winter, with temperatures down to minus seven degrees and some impressive storms. There were days when the time would drag, days when we would run out of the motivation to keep ourselves busy, days when the never-ending greyness of it all got us down. It was too much like a typical British winter but without any friends or work to help you take your mind off it.

This wasn't entirely unexpected. The structure of this new life was experimental and we had always thought that it might take us a year or two to get the mix right. From the few months spent on Olivia so far we knew this was something we wanted to keep doing, and for much longer than just one or two years. The new engine had put a hole in our coffers, plus we recognised that we needed to have more to do, so we decided that next winter we would go back to the UK and work for six months. That way we could keep our savings topped up and so afford to keep coming out for a good six months in the better weather, hopefully for many years to come.

Christmas Day arrived. We had bought ourselves a small tree and some lights and decorated Olivia. It took us all of two minutes to open our Christmas presents, none of which were surprises as it is hard to hide anything on a boat. We're not materialistic people and firmly believe that Christmas has become horribly commercial, but that morning it all felt rather anticlimactic. We realised that the ritual of waking up with family and gathering round a tree to share presents has been part of our lives since being toddlers. We missed it.

Our plan had been to spend a lazy morning indoors and then drive out to one of our favourite spots for a good stomp in the woods, saving our Christmas meal for the evening.

'It doesn't look very nice out there.' Michael looked dubiously at the leaden skies.

'We'll take waterproofs,' I said. 'I can't sit around here all day. I'll go stir crazy.'

The rain held off until we reached the furthest point from the van. The forest was sodden, puddles and squelchy, boot-grabbing mud everywhere. The colour palette was depressingly drab, shades of brown and grey, to the point where it felt as if all the colour had been sucked out of the world. We got soaked, the dogs got soaked and at some point on our miserable trudge back to the van we had to admit that this wasn't turning out to be our best Christmas ever.

Back on Olivia, we threw all our wet clothes into the bathroom and firmly shut the door on them, lit the wood burner, put a joint of pork and all the trimmings in the oven, and opened up a bottle of champagne. The meat needed a couple of hours cooking, so we opened up a second bottle and the world began to look much rosier. Our Christmas meal was delicious, three courses of fine dining so good that the overpowering smell of wet dog faded into the ether and disappeared.

'I love this stuff.' I twirled a glass of ratafia in my hand, nestled in my pile of cushions by the wood burner, watching the way the light caught the delicate ambers and golds, replete and content and doing my best to ignore the washing up piled around the kitchen sink.

'It wasn't such a bad day after all,' said Michael, topping up my glass.

'I'm not sure I want to do the same thing next Christmas though.'

'Probably not,' he agreed. 'We need to be at home with family. Or somewhere hot and sunny and totally different.'

'Like Bali,' I suggested.

'Works for me. But first a toast. To Olivia. To say thank you. There have been a few ups and downs, but I wouldn't be anywhere else right now. It's been a good first season.'

I clinked my glass against his and we smiled at each other. A good first season indeed.

PART THREE: 2018

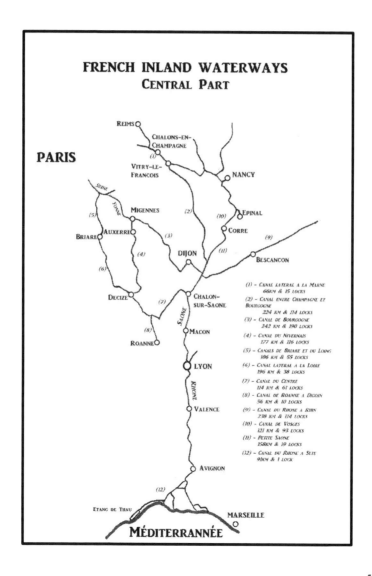

FRENCH INLAND WATERWAYS
CENTRAL PART

(1) - CANAL LATERAL A LA MARNE
       66KM & 15 LOCKS
(2) - CANAL ENTRE CHAMPAGNE ET
       BOURGOGNE
       224 KM & 114 LOCKS
(3) - CANAL DE BOURGOGNE
       242 KM & 190 LOCKS
(4) - CANAL DU NIVERNAIS
       177 KM & 116 LOCKS
(5) - CANALS DE BRIARE ET DU LOING
       106 KM & 55 LOCKS
(6) - CANAL LATERAL A LA LOIRE
       196 KM & 38 LOCKS
(7) - CANAL DU CENTRE
       114 KM & 61 LOCKS
(8) - CANAL DE ROANNE A DIGOIN
       56 KM & 10 LOCKS
(9) - CANAL DU RHONE A RHIN
       238 KM & 114 LOCKS
(10) - CANAL DE VOSGES
        121 KM & 93 LOCKS
(11) - PETITE SAONE
        158KM & 19 LOCKS
(12) - CANAL DU RHONE A SETE
        91KM & 1 LOCK

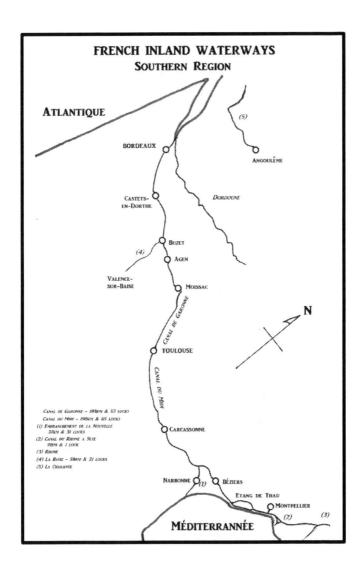

Chapter 8

A new season

We left Olivia briefly in early 2018, taking a month out to visit friends and family in the UK. Arriving back in Châlons-en-Champagne in late February, we found the boat held fast in thick ice that stretched the length of the canal for as far as we could see. The temperature was down to minus ten degrees centigrade but with the wind chill factor it seemed even colder, the air so sharp it felt as if it was slicing the skin from your cheekbones.

On some days the canal couldn't open until the lock-keepers had hacked away at the ice that had frozen the lock doors solid, and then it was up to the big commercial barges to do the serious work. Daggers of ice hung from the anchors suspended under their bows and, as they bulldozed their way through, the frozen canal broke apart in front of them, huge sheets of ice surging upwards as if in an earthquake and then subsiding again as they passed. Some days there were no boats at all and the canal was deserted save for the moorhens and coots, who skittered across the surface like clumsy ballerinas.

I hadn't seen this much frozen water since I was a child, when my parents took my brother and me out to the lakes near our home. I have a hazy memory of water frozen solid and people ice skating from one side to the other. It had been exciting then and it was exciting now, but it didn't stay that way for long. We wanted to leave and we couldn't move in this weather.

This compulsion to leave wasn't just because we were getting itchy feet. We were about to join the Canal entre Champagne et Bourgogne, which shut down for its annual maintenance session at the end of March. We needed to make sure we were clear of it before it closed, for we had a long journey planned for this year.

We were heading south, to the sun. Fair-weather boaters we may be, but the miserable winter had reinforced our opinion that the world feels a better place with a blue sky above your head and a warm sun on your skin. Our route would take us down two of the big rivers of France, the Saône and the mighty Rhône, right down to the south of France, across the Camargue and up the iconic Canal du Midi, finishing with the Canal de Garonne, which stops just short of Bordeaux. We would pass through the hearts of Toulouse, Avignon and Carcassonne on a journey of around 1,450 kilometres.

As we had only managed 588 kilometres in our short season in 2017, this seemed like a mammoth journey. Perhaps I should qualify that and say it is a mammoth journey *by boat* – it is obviously a quicker trip for those people hurtling down the motorways at speeds that are almost incomprehensible to us when we are on the water.

For ten long days we sat in the ice, breaking the days up by walking along the canal, cocooned in thick coats, our hats and scarves covering our faces so that only our eyes peered out. Like us, Olivia also waited for the ice to recede. Even when she is moored, she is rarely still. She moves as we move, rolling barely perceptibly as we shift our weight about the boat. The wash from a passing *péniche* sets her rocking gently, whilst a storm shifts the whole experience up a gear as the movement becomes more violent, pitching her from side to side.

Here in the ice she was unnaturally still, paralysed and held fast in its icy grip, and it felt wrong, as if the boat was no more than a husk and she had somehow left us. It was a relief when the ice finally thinned, and then reluctantly melted around us, and she came back to herself.

By March 5th we finally felt it was safe to leave. Our immediate stretch of canal wasn't totally ice free but it was thin enough for us to feel confident about getting through. The first time we turned the key and started up our new engine was a big moment. We had given it a short trial immediately after it was installed, and before the engineers left, but the real test of a job well done, hopefully without teething problems, would be proven over the coming months.

The ice may have largely melted from around Châlons-en-Champagne but as we climbed up towards the summit at Langres the temperature dropped, and it came back with a vengeance. There is nothing like the sound of ice splintering and cracking beneath your bow. It reverberated through the whole of the boat, a primeval, end-of-the-world sort of sound that had the dogs looking at us wide-eyed with fear, and us equally wide-eyed, wondering what damage we were doing to the hull or even whether we would eventually grind to a halt, locked in by the ice and unable to go any further. It was a relief once we reached the summit, began the descent and the ice disappeared.

The weather stayed wet and cold, with occasional bursts of sunlight to remind us that better days were to come. Most of the services at the moorings had been turned off because of the cold weather so it was hard to find anywhere with water to top up our drinking water tanks. They were big tanks, two of them holding 500 litres each, but we were wary of running out and so started to use water more sparingly. It didn't help that our water gauge, like so many things on Olivia, was on the blink, and gave us the same reading regardless of whether we were full or empty.

With no chance of hooking up to shore power we would normally have simply switched to our on-board diesel heating system. For some reason we had yet to understand, this was draining the house battery far faster than it should have, to the point where, unhappily, we had to give up on it. That meant our only source of heating was the wood burner, which kept us warm and cosy in the galley, but the warm air stopped just short of our bedroom door.

'It's not meant to be like this,' I grumbled to myself as we prepared for bed one night. 'I'm supposed to take clothes off to go to sleep, not put more of them on.' I pulled on my thickest pair of walking socks.

'Are you off out somewhere?' Michael replied, looked bemused.

'My feet were like blocks of ice last night.' I grabbed my woolly hat, rammed it down on my head, took a deep breath and forced myself and my thermals under the slightly damp duvet. We woke each morning to the walls and windows dripping with condensation, a result of our warm breath hitting cold surfaces.

We got so fed up with it we tried sleeping in the galley, next to the wood burner, where the dining room table folded down to make another double bed. It was not as comfortable as the bedroom and much narrower, so on one side you spent the night with your nose pressed up against the bookshelf and on the other you had a bird's eye view of the kitchen sink, but at least it was warmer.

The last straw came when the hot water system decided that it needed a few days off. The immersion tank was heated up by the engine as we cruised and after a cold day out on the canal and the prospect of a cold night in bed, the promise of a hot shower between the two had become one of the few pleasures of the day. Now, air was getting into the system, which meant it was a lottery as to whether we had hot water or not.

Despite the weather we had made good time down the canal, travelling 255 kilometres in 12 days and notching up 119 locks. We were ready for a change and were looking forward to getting onto the River Saône. Mooring opportunities were far fewer but there would be proper marinas with electricity and water.

Our final mooring point on the canal was at a place called Maxilly. Our intention was to stop here for one night and then make an early start on the river the following day. As per our normal evening ritual we took the dogs out for a walk, following the canal down to where it joined the river, to see what awaited us in the morning.

We heard it before we saw it. We stood high on the banks and looked down in disbelief at the River Saône, in full and glorious spate, roaring past us, wide and muddy and terrifying.

'We're not going on that, are we?' I asked faintly as an entire tree shot past me, carried so easily it could have been made of balsa wood.

'Not until it comes down.' Michael squinted at the far bank. 'I reckon that's at least five foot higher than it's supposed to be.'

We trudged back to Olivia and got in touch with the relevant VNF contact for this area. The river was shut to navigation. No boats were allowed on it until the levels went down and they had no idea when that would be. We just had to sit it out and wait.

There were times in this first rather trying month when I asked myself if I wished I were still back in Wales, living my old life, cosy and comfortable in a warm house where I took things like central heating and hot running water for granted. The answer always came back that I was right where I wanted to be. The pleasure I got from getting into a warm bed after several days of a cold one was intense. It was the same with a hot shower after days of going without. Feeling the sting of the rain on my face or the weak warmth of a winter sun as I threw my lines in the locks made me feel alive, closer to the natural world rather than shut away from it for most of the day.

Without all the systems we have built around ourselves to maintain the levels of comfort that most of us now believe are the natural order of things, we are a weak and vulnerable species. Being reminded of what it means to be human when a few of those systems are stripped away, even for a few days, was an enlightening experience.

Being on the water was also divesting me of any illusions I had about being in control of my life. There was no certainty that what we expected to do each day would be achieved by the evening. We would plan to overnight at a certain stop to find it completely decrepit and unusable when we arrived or, even more vexing, looking perfect but mysteriously chained off. The next mooring might be full of abandoned boats and the third option would be whatever we could get wherever we could get it. We might plan to do twenty kilometres in a day and end up doing half that because we got stuck behind a commercial barge going slower than a snail. And that was before you threw in ice or flood or storm.

That old cliché, going with the flow, eventually began to take on real meaning. There is no point in ranting against things that are completely outside your control, although it took me a while to accept this. At the ripe old age of fifty-seven, I had assumed I had fallen into the category of 'You can't teach an old dog new tricks', but with each month that passed, with each challenge overcome, I could sense something inside me was changing, and changing quite fundamentally, although it might only be me that realised it. I had undertaken this journey on Olivia to change my life, and perhaps it was naive not to foresee that my life and who I am are so closely connected that you can't alter one without changing the other. The way I looked at life, and the way in which I reacted to the various joys and vexations it threw at me was being subtly transformed, hopefully for the better.

Chapter 9

Let the rivers flow

It took five days for the water levels to recede to the point where the VNF were prepared to reopen the river to navigation. It had dropped at least five feet and was a quieter, tamer beast, but it wasn't a pretty sight. The flood waters had left the banks covered in thick, oozing mud and with the trees standing stark and bare, reaching skyward for warmth from a sun that kept its face resolutely hidden, the river seemed a cold and desolate place.

Although the water levels had dropped and the flow lessened, the floods had left a deadly legacy of floating driftwood that meant we had to be vigilant at all times. Short, chunky branches, perfect for snarling up the propeller, lay half-submerged, almost invisible until you were upon them, whilst twenty-foot long branches or even whole trees had to be dodged. If a big one hit us hard, or in the wrong place, it could put a hole in the hull.

The danger was still there even when we moored up for the night. Our first stop was at the marina in Chalon-sur-Saône, which was situated behind a small island just out of the main flow of the river. Boats visiting these larger marinas for short stays are usually given a mooring close to the entrance, rather than having a berth buried in the midst of all the long stay boats. You're not as sheltered from the elements but it makes it easier to get in and out.

The island provided some respite from the wash on the river, but there was still a substantial amount of driftwood coming through. We spent an hour or so watching it, trying to predict whose boat the next log was going to land against, occasionally leaping up with a boat hook to push one past us before it could get wedged between us and the pontoon.

'This is addictive.' I watched with satisfaction as a large branch sailed past, deftly diverted by my boat hook.

'Probably not in a good way,' said Michael. 'You won't be able to do that all night. Best we go out for a walk and forget about it.'

On our way out we chatted to some boat owners who had been there in January, only a couple of months before us, and they told us that the river had gone up so high that all the floating pontoons had risen to the top of the piles that anchored them in place. With commendable understatement they said it hadn't been fun. I craned my neck up and tried to imagine all the boats in this big marina six feet or more above my head, but imagination simply couldn't take me there. Even that paled into insignificance when compared to a flood of truly epic proportions which happened in 1840, when the river rose more than twenty-one feet.

After an evening of more boat-hook-versus-driftwood work we eventually went to bed, but sleep didn't come easily. The sounds of even a small branch thudding into the steel hull were magnified in the still of the night. Time after time I was on the point of dropping off and there would be another clunk. After a particularly loud, solid bang I elbowed Michael in the ribs.

'Wake up!'

'Why? What's happened?'

'That sounded like a massive branch.'

'What do you want me to do about it?'

'Go and look. Check everything's all right.'

'It'll be fine. Just ignore it.'

And in two seconds he was deeply asleep again.

We woke the next morning to find that Olivia had become a mini dam. She had two long branches, each over twenty feet long, wedged between her and the pontoon and these in turn had caught all the smaller stuff coming through. They had interwoven themselves in the way that only inanimate objects can, resulting in a dense, thick mat of wood. It took half an hour to clear it all, poking and prodding at the flimsier branches until they broke free and floated away. The biggest branches had somehow managed to get themselves twisted beneath the boat and it took the combined weight of both of us hanging on the end of a rope to yank them out.

If you look at a map of the canals and rivers in the top half of France it doesn't look that different to a road map, with various options taking you north, south, east and west. The bottom half of the map, beginning with the River Saône which then joins the Rhône, becomes almost a blank piece of paper, dissected by this single route that will take you south, a major artery that was used by commercial craft in much larger numbers than we had experienced so far.

The cargo-carrying *péniches* in this part of France would dwarf the ones we had come across on the northern canals. They were big enough to have their own on-board crane for the sole purpose of winching the barge owners' cars, often a his-and-hers pair of them, onto dry land in between shipments. The barges were so big they made the cars look tiny, like a child's toy collection and, as if they weren't intimidating enough by themselves, we would sometimes see two barges roped together, either in convoy or side by side. Even when fully loaded, they went at speed and stopped for no-one, their wash sending us lurching from one side of our boat to the other.

Both these rivers flow through popular tourist areas, particularly the wine-growing region in Burgundy, offering rich pickings for the luxury hotel boats, the other giant that we would have to get used to on this trip. We would regularly see the Lord

Byron shooting past us, several storeys high, its 140 passengers silhouetted through the windows as they were wined and dined at the cost of a mere £2,000 per person for a seven-day trip.

Both the Saône and the Rhône are canalised rivers, a term I had never heard of until we began our life on the water. As the name suggests it describes a hybrid of the two, with the locks placed at strategic points along the river to ensure sufficient depth of water for navigation. A canalised, man-made section of water, known as a *dérivation*, runs between locks until they reach a point where the depth in the river is sufficient to allow boats through again. The power of the water as it is shoehorned in through the locks, with unwanted water gushing over the weirs, is enormous and so these mighty rivers are harnessed at many of the biggest locks, their flow used to power hydroelectric stations.

We knew that the locks would be much bigger than any we'd seen so far, but even so the first one was a revelation. It was 185 metres long by 12 metres wide, big enough to comfortably hold 42 boats of Olivia's size.

With new locks came a new set of rules to learn, the most important one being that the commercial boats were the kings of the river and took precedence over all other, more lowly, forms of river traffic. They always went in first, filling the space like a bung in a bottle. There was usually room for a small boat like us to slip in behind them, a tiny David to their Goliath.

Whilst the lock-keepers on the canals were run ragged trying to manage a handful of locks, it was different on the rivers, where each lock had a set of full-time staff, co-ordinating and controlling the movement of all boats up and down stream.

There was a recognised procedure to follow. A couple of kilometres before we reached each lock it was my job to get on the VHF radio and tell them we were coming so that they could prepare the locks for us and advise us of any delay or problems. A small waiting pontoon was positioned outside the entrance so, if there was any delay, this was where we would moor up until we were told to proceed.

Once the lock was ready, either full or empty depending on which way we were going, the massive doors would grind slowly open, a red traffic light would turn to green and in we would go.

The communication ritual went something like this.

'Bonjour écluse de Seurre. Ici plaisancier Olivia Rose.'

There would be a wait of anything from a few seconds to a few minutes, usually with a round of static thrown in for good measure and then we would get a response.

'Oui. J'écoute.'

'Nous vous approchons et nous montons. On peut entrer?'

At this point the lines of communication became challenging as the response would invariably be a long one, delivered at great speed and buried in even more static.

'D'accord. Merci,' I replied.

'That went on a long time. What did he say?' asked Michael.

'I haven't got a clue. But the light has just gone green so we'll take that as a yes.'

We thought we'd got this sussed but then one morning, after the usual preamble, the light didn't go green. The doors had opened and towering, slab-sided walls awaited us, inviting as ever, but the light remained stubbornly red.

'Now what?'

'I'll try him again.'

'The answer came back promptly and in even greater detail than before, but I was still none the wiser. It was time to simplify things.

'Je suis désolée Monsieur mais je n'ai pas compris. Peut-on entrer, oui or non?'

'Non, Madame, non! Absolument pas!'

'Even I understood that,' said Michael. He turned and looked behind us. 'And that'll be the reason why.'

Powering up the river towards us was something we had not seen before. If most commercial barges are workhorses, battered and rough due to a hard life, then this was a thoroughbred which looked as if it had never done a day's work in its life. Its pristine decks gleamed like polished silver and shone so brightly in the sunshine that they hurt my eyes. The entire length of it was criss-crossed in an elaborate network of polished metal pipes, as well as vents and various other baffling protrusions. It looked like a floating factory but I couldn't begin to guess what it was for.

'What on earth is that?'

'I'm guessing it's a gas transporter. Or something like that. We've got a red light because they won't let us in the lock with it. Too dangerous. We'll have to wait for it to go and then they'll have to prepare the lock for us all over again.' Michael sighed. 'Another half an hour at least. I'll go and put the kettle on.'

One of our last stops on the Saône was in Mâcon, where we stayed for a few days as the weather had turned against us. High winds running against the flow turned the river into a mini sea, with white horses racing over the waves. We had taken shelter but the commercial traffic worked on tight schedules and didn't have that luxury. Even without the pressure of a deadline their engines were powerful enough to push through almost any weather. As usual the visitor moorings were on the outside pontoons so we took the brunt of the wash and the waves, Olivia's ropes straining to hold her fast.

The storm was due to peak in the early hours of the morning but it began to build up as we prepared our dinner. I watched, mesmerised, as the clouds darkened, turning from grey to black and sucking all the light from the sky. The water, ever a mirror for the heavens above, turned oily black and then exploded around us as the rain slammed into the surface like a million tiny meteors.

'This is going to be a big one,' said Michael.

I nodded, almost deafened by the rain pounding upon the roof of the boat and hurling itself against the windows. I love rainstorms. They are primeval. I imagine the gods grabbing handfuls of stars and hurling them earthwards with all their might, competing to see who can throw the furthest.

The thunder swept in after the rain, booming so deeply that I could feel it reverberating through my bones, the lightning tearing the sky apart. I closed my eyes and could still see it, the jagged rents of bright white imprinted on my eyelids. It lessened off eventually, but still circled around us, and we went to bed with a continuous background rumble, a promise that it wasn't over yet.

The storm reached its climax in the early hours and there was no sleeping through it. If the gods had been playful before their mood had now changed, becoming ugly and petulant. The gusts were so strong that the pontoons were bouncing up and down on the water. Olivia's ropes screamed and stretched to breaking point but thankfully they held. We watched as the boats around us were thrown from side to side, as flimsy and breakable as a child's toys, and were glad we couldn't see those same movements mirrored on Olivia. It felt bad enough inside the boat, as we stumbled about the galley, grabbing various kitchen items that were making a bid for freedom and trying without much success to calm the dogs, who plainly thought the world was crashing down upon them and that their end was nigh.

It seemed to go on for ever, rolling around and then coming in again, but eventually it tailed off and we managed to get some sleep, left both exhilarated and exhausted by the experience. Mostly we were just grateful we'd come through it in one piece.

I woke up the next morning, watched the swollen river surging past, and had a momentary longing to be back on the peace and tranquillity of the canals. This river felt unfriendly, as if we were riding upon a ravening beast, and I could imagine it licking its lips at the thought of chewing us up and spitting out what was left. Since we'd been on it we'd had floods, storms, and more flotsam and jetsam than I ever wanted to see again. Everything seemed oversized and intimidating and I felt as if I needed a few days of calm and respite before we joined the Rhône. Given that the two rivers merged in Lyons, only a few days away, I didn't think I was going to get it.

Although our experience of the Saône had been a bit too lively for comfort the river is, for much of the year, known for its benign nature. The Rhône, in contrast, is its mad, bad brother. Anyone who has 'done' this river has a story to tell, a rite of passage. When you mention that you're about to try your hand at it, they'll purse their lips, look mournful and wish you good luck.

There are good reasons to respect the Rhône. It is one of France's biggest rivers, powerful, unpredictable, and infamous for the strength of its currents. In spring heavy meltwater from the Alps swells the river and increases the flow, whilst in autumn heavy rainfall causes high water and flooding. Given that these two windows are when many pleasure boaters are on the water, either making their way south for the summer or for a warmer winter season on the Med, it is hard to avoid a potentially tricky passage. Navigation is further complicated because the hydroelectric generators create their own man-made currents and add significantly to the flow at certain times of the day. The Rhône Navigation Authority provides daily figures on flow rates with the aim of helping boats plan their journeys.

'So it says here that a *débit* is the flow of water in cubic metres per second.' I had my nose buried in our cruising guide. 'If we take a typical flow rate of 2,000 *débit* we need to multiply it by 0.0072 and that will give us the km/hour figure. That's when we're near Lyons. Once we get to Bourg-lès-Valence that figure changes to 0.0036. If the flow rate goes above 6,000 navigation is stopped.'

'What's it at now?'

'I'd have to go online to check. And it varies throughout the day because of the hydroelectric generators. They have their own peaks and flows. But I guess it's not so crucial for us anyway because we're going downstream. If the current is strong we just go faster. Olivia will turn into a speedboat and we'll be in the Med before you know it.' I had a happy warm glow at the thought.

'It's harder to control a boat going downstream in a strong flow,' warned Michael. 'You've got to line up your approach to the bridges far more carefully. If we bash into one of the supporting arches at speed, we'll damage the boat. Seriously damage her.'

Some of my happy glow faded a little. I returned to my reading.

'The other thing we have to look out for is the wind. Mainly the mistral, which apparently means "masterly", and usually comes from the north but not always. You can also get a strong south wind. We need to be aware of dangerous cross-currents between the locks and the barrages. We also need to look out for the big seagoing ships that can suck you in towards their stern so keep well away from them.' I snapped the book shut. 'I don't think I want to know any more. Looks like we just need to keep an eye on the weather, on the currents, on the other ships and try not to hit any bridges and we'll be fine.'

By the time we got to Lyons the weather had turned sunny again. The waterfront of this city, the third largest in France, is a diverse mix of ancient and modern. We cruised past terraces of imposing old town houses, five storeys high, mellow in shades of ochre and terracotta. On the opposite bank was a startling, lime green cube of a building, the headquarters for Euro News, garishly contemporary in design. A few minutes later we came across a structure of glass and concrete reminiscent of a spaceship. Lyons has been a settlement for over 2,000 years and I couldn't help but wonder what the Romans would have made of this modern version of their city.

A few moments later we arrived at the point where the Saône joins the Rhône, the two rivers merging so serenely that I was hardly aware it had happened. The city faded into the distance behind us and the landscape turned more industrial.

Then the engine stopped.

We both sat in disbelieving silence for a second or two until automatic reflex took over. Michael turned the key and she spluttered back into life.

I let out a long breath I didn't know I'd been holding. 'What happened there?'

'Don't know.'

The engine coughed once and stopped again. Olivia sailed merrily on but now she was controlled by her own momentum and the current, not by us. My brain refused to accept this was happening. It was a new engine, it had cost us so much money, and expensive new engines weren't supposed to go wrong.

'We need to find somewhere to moor up. And soon. I don't want to have to try and steer through a bridge in this flow without an engine.' Michael turned the key again but the result was the same and the look on his face made my stomach clench. I studied both banks but there was nowhere obvious for us to stop. The only possibility was a single commercial barge, moored up on an industrial dock ahead of us.

'I'll try and get us close to that barge. You'll have to get a line on it somehow.'

At first glance there didn't seem to be anybody on the barge and I wondered how on earth I was supposed to get a rope on with the current carrying us past so fast. I would only have one chance and I couldn't afford to miss. If there had been time to think about it I would have been utterly terrified but there was no time to think and some automatic, adrenalin-fuelled, life-preserving part of my brain kicked in.

I saw a faint shadow in the wheelhouse of the barge. It moved. I ran to our bow and waved my arms and yelled for help as loud as I could over the water.

'Au secours! Au secours!'

The shape moved closer to the window and I could just make out a coffee cup in its hand. I yelled again but the silhouette turned away. Another face appeared. A few seconds later a man came out on deck and just stood there, watching us. I couldn't believe it. I knew my French was good enough to be understood.

Whilst I was trying, and failing, to get their attention, Michael was lining Olivia up, using the current, and the odd surge from the engine before she failed yet again, to give us our best chance. I don't know what it was that finally brought some response from the men on the barge, whether it was me still jumping up and down, ever more furious at being ignored, or the fact that we were obviously coming in alongside them whether they liked it or not, but at last one of the men realised that something was wrong and started to run down the side of the boat towards us.

'I'll turn her so we're facing upstream and ferry glide her in,' Michael yelled at me. 'Get ready with a line.'

I grabbed a rope and gestured to the man on the boat that I would throw it to him. Michael spun the wheel fast, Olivia Rose turned a full hundred and eighty degrees and I threw the rope for all I was worth. The man on the barge grabbed it, tied it fast and we came alongside in what Michael later described as a 'controlled landing' but which to me felt as if it had more crash than control in it. The paint scratches were minimal though, so I guess he was right.

The man on the barge nodded at me and said something. I looked at him blankly. I had no idea what language he was speaking. Another man came up behind him, wiping greasy hands on a rag, and between the two of them they managed to explain that they were part of a crew of Lithuanians and Russians, carrying out maintenance checks on the barge. They spoke a little English but hardly any French, which explained why it took them so long to realise what was going on. They were burly, heavyset men, not overly given to smiling or chatting, and obviously not particularly interested in our plight, but they weren't leaving until tomorrow so they said we could stay rafted up against them until then if need be. We thanked them profusely and we all got on with what we had to do.

I knew things were serious when Michael got the engine manual out. Manuals only ever came out as a last resort.

'Do you have any idea what's gone wrong?'

'I think it's a problem with fuel getting to the engine.'

We worked through a menu of possible causes. Our fuel gauge was very erratic so it was possible that we had run out of fuel. We doubted this as we kept a strict record of our daily consumption just so that this sort of thing didn't happen, but we had a spare twenty litre tank of diesel on board so we put it in anyway. The engine fired up and stayed running. We looked at each other in disbelief. It couldn't be that easy. And indeed it wasn't as the engine died again after less than sixty seconds.

'We must have a blockage. But God knows where it is.'

'Why don't we call Nick?' I suggested. Nick was the engineer who had installed our engine for us. 'He always said if we had a problem to come back to him.'

So we called Nick and he talked through a list of possible causes and the remedies. He also thought it was most probably a blockage, possibly air in the system, or a bit of dirt sucked up from the fuel tank that had got through the filters. Michael ended the call and sighed. 'I need to work my way through the whole system, bleeding each component as I go to make sure the fuel is getting through and then it needs to be reprimed.'

'Have you done this before?'

'Nope.' He pulled the engine instruction manual over. 'Bit more reading required.'

The next couple of hours were spent methodically working through the fuel system, a crash course in engine maintenance. I watched my calm, resourceful, endlessly patient husband and blessed him. He happened to look up as I was thinking these thoughts and something must have showed in my face.

'What have I done wrong now?' He grinned and wiped a grubby hand across his forehead.

'Nothing major. Fancy a cup of tea?'

'Thought you'd never ask.'

A word of advice to any prospective fellow female boaters – if you don't have a partner who can turn his hand to anything and if, like me, you are not an experienced engine mechanic yourself, I should choose an adventure that keeps you on dry land.

An hour or so later the engine had been bled, sucked, flushed and primed and finally stayed running for more than a few seconds. We let her run for a good fifteen minutes as a test.

'This can't happen again, can it?' I needed the reassurance of knowing that this absolutely, definitely could never be repeated, but I should have known better.

'Theoretically it can happen at any time. A bit of air getting in where it shouldn't or a bit of dirt from the bottom of the tank is all it takes. But I think she's all right now. We just have to cast off and see how it goes. Are you ready to let those lines go?'

'Not really.' I felt like a reluctant limpet being prized off a big, sturdy, safe rock. But it had to be faced. The Lithuanians and Russians had all disappeared so we couldn't say goodbye or thank you. We just cast off and hoped for the best.

Thankfully the engine behaved and we made it to our mooring for that evening without further drama.

I lay in bed that night, listening to Michael breathing slow and deep beside me, and had a massive attack of the 'what ifs'.

What if there had been no commercial barge to tie up against? What if the engine had cut out under a bridge and we had crashed into one of the arches? What if it had happened right in the path of a hotel boat and they had crashed into us?

All my 'what ifs' ended with either Olivia being badly

damaged or us drowning. Or both. I'm scared of the water and drowning has always been top of my list for one of the many ways that I don't want to die. I gave myself a stiff talking to. None of those things happened. We made it through in one piece and that was all that mattered.

'But what if you weren't so lucky next time?' whispered the nasty little demon that resides in my head.

'I'm not going to worry about some fictional next time that may never happen,' I retorted. 'I've sorted all that stuff out. I don't worry about things any more.'

The demon sniggered as if it knew better and I had a restless, uneasy night.

Chapter 10

La Bollène

We decided to try and finish the last ninety kilometres of the Rhône in one push. It would make for a long day, but safe moorings were in short supply, the few that were available often situated on exposed sections of river. It would have been unthinkable to attempt this sort of distance in one day on the canals but we had a strong flow behind us and a manageable number of locks to get through. The biggest of these was a lock called La Bollène.

As the highest mountain peaks gain their status and symbolism simply because they are the biggest, so La Bollène has a similar reputation in the boating world. With this one under our belts, all others would pale into insignificance.

La Bollène was the biggest lock in the world at the time it was built in 1952. It is twenty-three metres deep, equivalent to the height of a seven-storey building. One of the locks on the Danube, at thirty metres deep, has now claimed the world record but, to my mind, when you've got that much concrete towering above you another few metres is neither here nor there.

La Bollène took five years to build, used 600,000 cubic metres of concrete and produced 50 million cubic metres of excavations. I had expected that it would take ages to fill up or empty but, astonishingly, it takes only seven minutes due to an ingenious system of 'bottom filling'. Although this sounds like an unpleasant medical condition, it actually refers to the system that allows the lock to fill from underneath the boats, with the water being pushed up at speed through a series of outlets along the length of the lock.

Locks are dangerous places. Huge amounts of water are either gushing in or out at speed, creating both vertical and horizontal currents, as well as whirlpools which well up underneath you. Your chances if you fall in are not good. Accidents do happen, but these huge locks are so finely controlled that they often feel safer than the smaller locks, where the flow of water can be erratic and throw the boat all over the place. However, in 2001 someone died in an accident in La Bollène, a terrible reminder that every lock demands respect.

We were travelling downstream so this meant that we entered the lock when it was full. Life jackets are mandatory, as is securing the boat to a bollard. In these deep locks we tie up to what are known as floating bollards, a bollard that is inset into a channel in the lock wall and which descends at the same rate as the boat, hence the term 'floating'. Once the lock-keeper can see everyone is safely secured, the doors close and the waters go down.

Sometimes seven minutes can fly by, other times they don't. The lower we got, the slower the clock ticked. I craned my neck back as far as it would go and still all I could see were grey, slab-sided walls stretching ever upwards to a tiny rectangle of sky that got smaller and smaller. The deeper we got the colder it became, as the sun didn't reach this far down.

Ladders were fixed to the walls, providing an emergency exit if something should go wrong. I tried to imagine how it would feel to abandon Olivia and trust my weight to such a flimsy looking structure, its metal rungs slippery and cold under my fingers.

I caught Michael's eye and he grinned in delight from the other end of Olivia. 'Isn't this great?'

Given the fact that we spend literally twenty-four hours a

day together we are fortunate in that we are in tune most of the time, but it is in situations like this that I realise we view the world quite differently. Luckily, I knew he didn't need much of an answer. 'Yes dear', said with as much conviction as could be mustered, would suffice.

Time might go slowly but it can't ever stop, and so our seven minutes eventually passed, the doors cranked reluctantly open and out we came.

At some point in that last ninety kilometres, a miracle occurred. The air changed, becoming soft against our skin. The trees lining the banks, their branches previously peppered with just a hint of green, seemed to burst forth overnight. The sky turned sapphire blue and I lifted my face towards it, a human sunflower, unable to resist the warmth against my skin. Our world of grey and black, of wind and rain, faded as if it had never been. We cruised into Avignon, our final port on the Rhône, in a time warp, as if we had arrived in summer, bypassing spring completely.

I could feel a wave of exhausted euphoria washing over me. This trip had pushed me well out of my comfort zone but it had been worth it. You could spend a lifetime on boats and still have much to learn, but I felt as if I had taken a credible first step towards becoming more proficient. It was a good feeling.

The port of Avignon is situated up a side-arm of the river, sheltered from the wash and the flow, and right in the heart of the city. We could see the walls of the old town, criss-crossed with alleyways, tourists eating and drinking out on the pavements, but we were too tired to join them. It would all be there in the morning.

Just before we went to bed a WhatsApp came through from friends back in Wales. They'd sent us a picture of themselves out walking in the hills, dressed in full winter gear, even down to the woolly hats, hunched against a glowering April sky.

We nobly resisted the impulse to send them a picture of our blue-sky day and fell into bed.

In the early hours of the morning a woman screeched outside the boat. We both sat bolt upright, hearts pounding, jolted from a deep sleep and completely disorientated. There was another voice, a man's. He shouted at her, she screamed back at him and we peered anxiously through the slats in our bedroom blinds, wondering if we had time to get dressed before rushing out to save a damsel in distress. After a few seconds we realised that it was the man who might need rescuing. There was a lot of finger pointing, foot stomping and pacing to and fro but it didn't look as if anybody was in mortal danger.

'I think it's best if we let them work through it.' I flipped the slats shut and flopped back on the bed. 'I just hope they sort themselves out soon.'

'This wouldn't happen back home.' Michael pummelled his pillow. 'A bit of British restraint wouldn't go amiss.'

'It's just the French being French. All fire and passion.' I yawned. 'But I wouldn't mind if they kept their passion indoors where it doesn't disturb other people.'

The shouting got progressively quieter but we were asleep before they finally left. I have no idea whether it ended with reconciliation or with broken hearts.

Chapter 11

Avignon

We woke late the following morning to the luxurious feeling of knowing we didn't have to be anywhere by any set time. We had our usual morning cup of tea, and then we treated ourselves to another one while we took stock of our surroundings. Given that Avignon is such a major tourist attraction, the port is quite a small one, with a large share of the moorings taken by hotel boats, not the giants from the main river, but still much bigger than us. We had been lucky to get a spot. In high season the boats are apparently rafted up three or four deep, but in early April it was still relatively quiet so we didn't have to share our berth.

Mooring fees were €27 per night, expensive but not unexpected given its prime location. They obviously wanted you to stay as they had an offer of pay for four nights and you get the next three for free. We thought we might do that, our only niggle being the proximity of the ring road, four lanes of constant traffic immediately adjacent to the quay. It was controlled by traffic lights so we got into the habit of saying what needed to be said in the lull between the reds and the greens, otherwise we could hardly hear ourselves speak.

The Palais des Papes is the largest Gothic palace ever built.

It was constructed by Pope Clement V in 1309 and now attracts approximately 650,000 visitors annually. I would love to have seen Pope Clement's face if he could have joined us as a present-day tourist, for his former seat of power has been given a makeover on a scale he could never have imagined.

Once the good pope had paid his €12 at the ticket office, he would be shepherded to a second reception desk which would issue him with an augmented reality iPad, described as a 'Histopad', and a set of headphones, with the commentary available in seven different languages. Proceeding through the Audience Hall to the Papal Chamber or the Consistory, he would log in to a centralised docking station in each room, then scan the tablet slowly around. At this point I found myself hoping that the good pope had been lucky enough to catch a couple of episodes of *Doctor Who* before his visit today. If not it was going to be a steep learning curve, for life had moved on in the last 700 years. As the Histopad scanned the room the screen would show a simulation of what each room would have looked like in its prime, with rich tapestries and priceless frescoes adorning the walls, even banqueting tables laid out for a sumptuous feast.

The Palais des Papes was extensively sacked and looted during the years of the French Revolution. In 1791 it became a military barracks and a prison and many of the rooms were whitewashed. Looking back, this seems to have been an astonishing act of vandalism. Although a comprehensive programme of restoration is ongoing, certain areas remain stark and bare to this day, so I can understand why they have felt the need to recreate what has been lost.

But I wished they'd found a different way to do it.

I looked around me and all I could see were people staring fixedly at their iPad screens, arms outstretched at shoulder height as they scanned slowly around the room, headsets clamped to their ears. No-one spoke. Each face had that particular expression of inward concentration that is an unmistakeable symptom of exposure to modern-day technology.

It was surreal. I wondered if I had blundered into a film set for some futuristic science fiction vision of what life holds for the next generations of humanity, but then I realised that there was nothing futuristic about this. Welcome to the digital age.

'This is horrible,' I whispered to Michael. 'No-one is actually looking at what is in front of them. No-one is talking about what they're seeing. They're just staring at a screen like zombies.'

He couldn't hear me. Like everyone else, he was absorbed in the headphone commentary. I looked around to see if I was the only one who was not enthralled by this new technology, and it seemed I was.

So be it.

I took my headphones off, stuffed the tablet in my bag and made a mental note to myself not to walk out without giving it back. The use of the iPad was included in the ticket price, but there was definitely an expectation that it would be returned before you could leave. The rest of my visit took place using my imagination rather than a simulation. A small, probably quite meaningless, personal protest against the way the world is going, but it made me feel better.

The following morning found us out on our bikes, heading away from the crowds on a forty-mile round trip to Pont du Gard. Our route wound its way through old, rural France, unchanged for years and exuding a sense of comforting permanency that was a world away from roaring traffic and virtual reality living.

We cycled through hamlets and past isolated farmsteads, paint peeling off crooked wooden doors and rusty tractors parked up in old stone barns. Wisteria pushed insistent tendrils into tiny gaps in stonework, or entwined itself around archways. Time and again I would catch a hint of its sweet scent as I freewheeled past. The land was a green and brown patchwork quilt, split into countless small plots. Vines were just coming into leaf, planted with military precision, row after row marching along until they were brought up short against a hedge or a fence. Everywhere we looked we saw fruit trees: apples, pears, cherries and plums. The sense of abundance, of the irrepressible, pulsating cycle of life, was overwhelming and I could picture the rich bounty of the harvest to come.

Eventually the neat orderliness of farmland gave way to trees and open spaces, unruly and wild, with streams tumbling and leaping over boulders. I knelt by the bank, listening to the bird song, and trailed my fingers though the cold, clear water. All my senses, sight, sound, smell and touch, were intensely aware, completely tuned in to the natural world.

An image of the tourists trudging through the gloomy depths of the Palais des Papes flashed briefly into my mind and was just as quickly banished. In contrast to the sense of life all around me, so animated, so vital, those silent halls seemed a dead space. I believe there is nothing that man can build or invent that matches the natural world. If I want to experience a moment of pure contentment, a sense of absolute rightness, this is where I find it.

Having said that, the Pont du Gard is truly impressive. Spanning the River Gardon in graceful arches three tiers high, this ancient Roman viaduct is a worthy testament to man's ingenuity, not just because it was built so long ago and yet still stands largely intact, but also because it has a serene beauty to it. Each arch framed a different picture of sky, river and trees, and the effect was that it seemed part of the landscape, rather than apart from it.

Despite a constant stream of visitors, the Pont du Gard is a tranquil spot, with the visitor centre and a small café situated at the entrance, well away from the aqueduct itself. We bought an ice-cream and found some flat rocks to sit on, the stone warm beneath our bare feet. Big fish, easily two feet long, swam lazily in the river below us, disappearing into the weeds with a lazy twitch of a powerful tail whenever the shadow of a bird passed overhead.

The next day we cycled out to the tourist village of St Remy, charming and chic, exclusive and expensive, part of the day-tripping itinerary for the big seagoing cruise ships docked in Marseille. American accents were everywhere.

We ordered a coffee and a *pâtisserie* from a small pavement café and indulged ourselves in a session of shameless people-watching.

'Why have they all got little round sticky labels on their clothes?' I peered at an American couple coming out of a *fromagerie* across the street.

'These are passengers from cruise ships.' Michael grimaced

as he always did whenever anything triggered memories of his time aboard this particular type of ship. Even the most exotic of places can become ordinary when you've navigated round them ten times with nearly three thousand passengers for company. 'That number on the label is so they know which coach to get back on.'

I looked more closely as a steady procession of 'labelled' people walked past us. It is fair to say that they were all of retirement age, some of them almost out the other side.

'I hope I can still remember who I am and where I'm going when I finally get to draw my pension,' I said fervently. 'If not, it's your duty as my loving husband to put a pillow over my head.'

If the number of designer carrier bags full of goodies were anything to go by, then St Remy was making a good living from the cruise ship business.

'That woman has got eight bags of shopping.' I watched as a well-endowed, heavily wrinkled woman with a somewhat younger man in tow lowered herself into a chair at a table opposite. 'It must have cost a fortune.'

'That's nothing,' said Michael. 'They'll go to the casino every night on board ship and lose five or ten thousand pounds. That's where the cruise liner companies make their money.'

We left the Americans to their buying frenzy and headed for the hills. Our real destination today was Les Alpilles, a chain of jagged mountains strung between the rivers Rhône and Durance. We had read that it was a biking and walking paradise, criss-crossed with trails, and promising spectacular views once you had sweated your way to the top.

Whilst I am a keen walker, venturing into the high hills on two wheels is not something I would ever have dreamed of doing until I invested in an electric bike. It has given me the confidence to go almost anywhere and I am not alone in having made this discovery.

Electric bike sales are rocketing across the globe. In Europe, it is the Netherlands which has seen the largest take-up, with electric bikes outselling conventional varieties, but we saw them everywhere in France as well.

Today, however, the only electric bike up on the summits of Les Alpilles was mine. We saw no-one else apart from a few walkers in the far distance and it was easy to imagine that all this grandeur was here for our benefit alone. It's at times like this that I am reminded how big France is, how easy it is to escape from people and lose yourself in its wildness.

We got back down a great deal faster than we got up, arriving at the bottom flushed and exhilarated. A couple of hours later we arrived back in Avignon, swinging off our bikes and walking them past the busloads of tourists endlessly convening outside the Palais des Papes until we reached the quay. Olivia was there waiting for us and I was struck yet again by what a beautiful boat she is. At some point in the future perhaps I will take all this for granted, but right now I am still regularly overcome with a sense of wonder that this is our life.

Chapter 12

Living in small spaces

'I know there's a tin of beans in here somewhere.' I was down on my hands and knees in front of one of the kitchen cupboards, peering into the depths.

'Try this.' Michael passed me the head-torch.

'That's better. Maybe just there …' Our cupboards are so deep that I practically have to climb in to find things at the back, fingertips outstretched and scrabbling to gain purchase on things that don't want to be found. We usually had a baguette and a selection of French cheeses and fruit for lunch, but today I had an urge for fried egg and baked beans on toast.

'Any luck?'

I inched the tin towards me until I could read the label. 'Not really. Unless you fancy fried egg and chick peas?'

There is an art to managing the practicalities of life when you live in a relatively small space and we hadn't yet fully mastered it. It requires organisation and discipline, with every item having its set place. Wasting this precious space by hanging on to unnecessary items is one of the cardinal sins of the boating ethos, and so I had developed a ruthless streak. That coat I hadn't worn for two years had to go. So did a set of eight champagne flutes. And we only needed four mugs, two for us and two for guests, not the twelve mugs we'd had in the days when we owned a dishwasher.

It took a few months to re-educate my brain but I found it surprisingly satisfying. If accumulating possessions is a modern-day addiction, the reverse process is equally compulsive. There is an invigorating sense of freedom in owning so little, and yet it being all that you need. Having to fit all your worldly goods into a boat thirteen metres long and three and a half metres wide concentrates the mind and forces you to prioritise what really matters. We moved from a four-bedroomed house and I don't miss a thing.

My one weakness is books. Most of my reading is done on a Kindle, but the lure of a bookshop is irresistible. It hurts to come out empty-handed. Luckily we have a small bookshelf on board, so every now and then I give in and indulge myself.

A tougher challenge is tidiness. There simply isn't the space to get something out of a cupboard and not put it back when you've finished with it. We're both naturally untidy people but boat-living was slowly remoulding our habits.

The design of boats is a fascinating thing. It requires a practical creativity to make the most out of every single inch of space. Getting the balance right is important, as the result has an impact on how you relax and sleep as well as how you store things. Not all boats are created equal in this regard. The wide Dutch barges are very capacious, easily accommodating a three-piece suite and a kitchen the same size as a modest house. We have seen some with hot tubs on deck and others with hotel-style en-suite bedrooms. These old boats can be full of character but they felt too big for us, like a house that just happens to be floating on the water.

At the other end of the scale, some friends of ours have taken a two-year break from work to sail their twenty-six foot catamaran on an epic journey down the Danube and through the Mediterranean. They squeeze themselves into the hulls to sleep, and cook in the space one person can stand up in. Olivia lies in the middle ground between these two extremes, small enough to feel like a proper boat but big enough to allow comfortable living.

Even this middle ground requires a different mindset. There is no free-standing furniture. Comfy chairs are replaced by benches that double up as spacious lockers. The area beneath our bed has been converted into two huge, pull-out drawers. The galley table and bench seats fold down to make a second double bed. A safe has been cunningly hidden behind what seems to be just another piece of panelling. A wooden panel at the bow end, adjacent to the anchor locker, can be unscrewed to reveal a cavernous space for storing bigger items that we don't need on a regular basis. A wedge-shaped area under the kitchen work surface is impractical for most things, but perfect for a wood store.

Moving from the land to the water means you gain a boat but lose a garden. I love flowers and growing plants from seed and was determined not to give up on this just because we had no land. My pot collection grows every month. My current tally stands at nineteen, with a third of them arranged at the bow. These contain strawberries and my herb collection – parsley, chives, mint, rosemary, basil and coriander. Geraniums and petunias tumble in profusion from window boxes, deep velvety-purple and soft rose-pink, whilst mange-tout and tomato plants clamber up a rather spindly home-made trellis on the top deck. There is a long-standing tradition amongst boat owners of having flowers on board. If there were prizes for such things, Olivia would be up there with the best of them.

The buying and storing of food was yet another area that had to be adapted to suit our situation. During our time in Wales we had a smallholding. For seven years we enjoyed a larder filled with home-made jams and chutneys, vegetables from our allotment, meat from our sheep and pigs and a steady supply of eggs from the chickens. If the world had come to an end we wouldn't have starved – for a while at least.

The habit of having plentiful stores doesn't work on a boat for two reasons. Firstly, there isn't the space to hoard. Secondly, we go shopping on foot, or on the bikes. We can buy only what will fit inside our rucksacks, our bike panniers and our little bike-trailer. This turned out to be a highly efficient system for making sure we only bought what was on the shopping list. It also made shopping a far more pleasant experience, an outing in its own right rather than a chore to be got over with as soon as possible.

'Stop it,' Michael hissed in my ear.

'Stop what?'

'You've been staring at that woman for ages.'

'I'm not staring at her. I'm staring at what she's bought.'

'It's just meat.'

'It's a mountain of meat. You could feed a family of ten for a month with that lot.' I gazed at the ever-growing pile of inch-thick steaks, strings of sausages, a slab of pale and, to my English eyes, rather disgusting tripe, burgers, pâtés and pies. 'It's going to cost a fortune.'

Michael looked embarrassed and wandered off. We were in a French market, one with leanings towards the *artisanale* end of the scale, selling local delicacies to die for at prices designed to help you on your way.

I moved a little closer as the lady finally got her purse out of her bag. The bill came to €130. The same thing happened with a different lady on the fish stall. She bought €60 worth of fish, whilst a man at the *boulangerie* counter bought twenty mini pastries. By now I was beginning to feel a bit like some weird food-stalker and I had a feeling that people were staring at me so I moved off and went in search of Michael.

'You'll never believe how much those people have spent on food.'

'I could hazard a guess. Look at these *tartes.* I was going to buy us a couple until I saw the price.' He sounded aggrieved. '€8 each. Each! I'd finish one in just three bites.'

On this occasion we left the market empty-handed. There is a popular conception, often misplaced, that anyone who owns a boat is wealthy. We certainly aren't, and we met many others like us who were doing something they loved, but on a shoestring. We very quickly learnt that France can be expensive for food. If we wanted to stick to our weekly budget we had to shop sensibly and we did this by sticking rigidly to what was on the shopping list and resisting impulse buys – at least that was the theory of it. We always supported the local *boulangerie* whenever we could as they are struggling to survive in some rural areas.

Perhaps some elements of this way of living might sound frugal, but we never felt that any of it was a hardship. If anything, quite the reverse was true. We had stumbled upon an incredibly healthy lifestyle, a perfect combination of fresh air, exercise and good food. Neither were the benefits restricted to a purely physical sense of well-being. With each week that passed I could feel my busy mind emptying, becoming a quieter, calmer place. The endless round of decisions that have to be made in normal life, and that cause such pressure and stress, fade away on a boat. Life becomes pared down, simple and yet richer because of it. If doctors could prescribe two weeks on a boat, to be taken at regular intervals, once a year every year, the world would be a happier, healthier place.

Chapter 13

To the Mediterranean

From Avignon the Rhône splits into two – the Grand Rhône wends its way south-east, while the Petit Rhône is, as the name suggests, a much less threatening affair, hardly wider than a canal. Impenetrable, tree-lined banks gave it a lush, closed-in feel after the expanse of the main river.

Two hours later we turned off and joined the Canal du Rhône à Sète, a seventy-four kilometre stretch passing through the Camargue, land of the famous wild white horses, on its way to the Mediterranean.

The Camargue is described as the 'Wild West' of France. I imagined vast, dusty plains with cowboys sleeping out under the stars, but in reality the Camargue is Western Europe's largest river delta, a vast plain indeed but a wet one, made up of large brine lagoons, or *étangs*, which are cut off from the sea by sandbars. It is a haven for birds and insects, famous for its pink flamingoes and black bulls as well as the white horses and, rather more infamously, home to some ferociously enthusiastic mosquitoes. There are 3,500 species of mosquito in the world, 49 of which inhabit the French Mediterranean. It is only the females who bite, as they need blood to sustain their eggs through to hatching, but I fear this fascinating fact is unlikely to make anyone who has been feasted upon feel better.

The horses are used by *gardiens*, or cowboys, to round up the black bulls, and so I assume this must be why some enterprising marketing guru made a link to the Wild West, but it seems a weak one, and unnecessary as there is much else of interest here.

We moored up in a small marina in the village of Gallician for our first night, swapping the roar of the city traffic in Avignon for a deafening cacophony of croaking and chirping from the crickets, frogs and who knows what else that filled the reed beds and marshes around us. It was hard to believe that such little critters could make so much noise and that it could carry so far. I discovered that I could sleep through this quite happily and, much to our surprise, we didn't get a single mosquito bite either.

I had read that the French have been doing battle with the mosquitoes for years, firstly using a natural insecticide on the insect larvae that had some success initially, but then was found to have negative effects on the surrounding food chain, and more latterly with a sort of bespoke vacuum cleaner which used carbon dioxide to lure them into a tube. I don't think either of these methods ever really stood a chance given the sheer numbers that nature throws at us in this situation. We were just lucky to be passing through early in the season, before they'd got into their blood-sucking stride.

We left the next morning and found a different infestation along the canal banks, a man-made one this time.

'That's seen better days,' said Michael, slowing down to look at an old wreck of a car abandoned by the side of the canal. It was covered in a muddy sludge, gutted and deformed by fire, with what was left rusted and full of holes. It could only have come out of the canal and I wondered what would have happened to our propeller if we had driven over it.

It seemed strange that somebody would deliberately dump a car in a canal, but a few miles further on we saw another, then another, all in a similar state. The VNF were obviously in the midst of a major clean-up operation because, by the end of the day, we had seen a total of five wrecked cars. We had intended to enjoy a few nights' wild-mooring along the quieter stretches of this canal, but the prospect of sharing them with a bunch of car thieves wasn't exactly appealing. Instead we spent the next night at Maguelonne, moored in splendid isolation on a vast long quay that would be crammed full of boats in high season. A fifteen-minute walk found us on the beach and enjoying our first swim in the Med.

'It's April 24th and I'm swimming in the sea,' I said.

'It's April 24th and twenty-eight degrees,' said Michael. We grinned happily at each other.

The next day we passed through the lifting bridges in Frontignan, heading towards the Étang de Thau. This is a vast stretch of water, twenty-one kilometres long and eight kilometres wide, but quite shallow, between five and ten metres in depth for the most part. It is separated from the sea by no more than a spindly sandbar so whilst it is technically a lake, it felt more like the sea, and was certainly wild enough when the wind got up. The wind was too strong on the day we arrived, making it dangerous to cross, and so we had to wait it out.

The next day dawned fair, perfect conditions, the water and the sky merging together, stretching from the horizon to the heavens. It seemed as if our whole world had turned intensely, gloriously blue. Olivia's bow sliced through indigo-blue water, scattering diamonds in her bow wave where the sun caught the spray. I lay out full length on the deck, the sky cornflower blue above me, the sun hot on my face, and was overcome by a rush of pure joy. This was freedom.

This stretch of water has provided ideal conditions for oyster and mussel production for centuries, dating as far back as the Greeks. They are grown in floating wooden platforms, with the French typically proud of their history and their purity, but it's not an easy life being an oyster.

The baby oysters are cemented onto long lengths of heavy-duty string, and then plunged into the water. There is an art to how they are positioned, and also the timing of their submersion, so as to avoid being eaten by anything other than us. At some point they are hoisted back up again, pulled off the string, spread out to allow room for further growth and recemented in position.

It takes up to a year for them to reach maturity.

Despite the widely-held belief that they are an aphrodisiac, there is no proof that this is actually true. However, they are rich in zinc, which promotes energy and vitality. If you combine a bit of wishful thinking of a sexual nature into that sudden hit of energy it might explain where the story came from.

Leaving oysters and thoughts of lively libidos behind us, we would now begin a major new phase of our journey, cruising along the 525 kilometres of waterway known as the Canal des Deux Mers. This actually consists of two canals, the famous Canal du Midi, and the lesser known Canal de Garonne. The two seas that the title refers to are the Mediterranean, where we would begin, and the Bay of Biscay on the Atlantic, although the canal itself stops just short of the ocean, fifty kilometres from Bordeaux.

The Canal du Midi is a World Heritage Site, much loved by boaters, cyclists and walkers, as well as those who live along it. It was built by Pierre-Paul Riquet, who solved the problems of ensuring a reliable supply of water by creating the Bassin de St Ferréol, a huge dam and reservoir and the largest man-made lake in the world at the time. Construction began in 1667 and it officially opened in 1681. It was a daunting task, his life's work and great passion, and he poured every last penny of his considerable fortune into turning his dream into a reality. He died a few months before the Grand Opening. I wonder what thoughts went through his head as he lay on his deathbed.

The first few kilometres of the Canal du Midi were not what we expected. A higgledy-piggledy assortment of boats lined the narrow channel, making it difficult for boats to pass. A few of them were securely moored and well maintained, but many looked as if their owners had thrown any old rope at the bank and hastily disappeared. Some boats had been left in this state for so long that they were now half-submerged, tipped awkwardly on their side, an ungainly, unnatural position for a boat, with their innards exposed and water turning everything to rust and ruin.

Some of the boats looked as if people had lived on them in the past, rickety wooden picnic tables left abandoned on deck, cracked and faded flower pots that hadn't seen a geranium in years, and piles of rubbish both inside and outside the boat, to the point where some of them looked like floating scrapyards. Occasionally we would see movement inside these wrecks and wonder who could live in such chaos. It certainly made for interesting cruising and perhaps they had a neglected charm to them – or perhaps we were trying too hard and they were just neglected.

We had a new breed of locks to get to grips with on the Midi, oval-sided rather than the more practical straight sides we were used to, and also a new breed of boater to share the waterways with – the holiday rental boater.

There is no mistaking a rental boat. They are white and plastic, often dented and scratched, and the person standing at the helm will probably never have been on a boat before and so spends most of his, occasionally her, time veering chaotically from side to side, bashing into lock gates, ricocheting off mooring walls and inducing terror in any boat unlucky enough to get in their path. I am aware that I am tarring all holiday boaters with the same brush, which isn't exactly fair, but there are so many of them that fall into this category that it is at least a partial truth.

In France, anyone can hire a boat without any prior experience whatsoever. Often, the only instruction given is via a short video, although some of the more reputable hire companies will take the intrepid mariners out on the boat itself for half an hour before turning them loose. For those of us who own our own boat it is a completely different situation, with strict requirements that we must have the necessary qualifications, and the paperwork to prove it.

There are good reasons for this. Controlling a boat isn't as easy as it might look, particularly if the wind gets up or if you are manoeuvring in a tight space. A boat out of control can do a lot of damage, to itself and to others, and so turning people out onto the water so ill-prepared seems astonishing, if not downright immoral.

Some people get the hang of it quickly, coming back year after year because it genuinely is a great way to get out on beautiful waterways without the expense of owning your own boat but, judging from the horror and naked panic that was a regular feature on the faces of other people, many do not find it at all easy. A honeymooning couple had such a bad time of it that they literally dumped the boat after forty-eight hours and walked away. Hopefully their marriage lasted longer than their holiday.

To put the other side of the case, without these holiday rentals the canals simply could not survive. The rental companies pay a very substantial licence fee for their boats, which goes towards maintaining the canal system. The holiday makers come from all around the world – French, British, Russians, Germans, Italians, Americans, Australians, New Zealanders or South Africans – and are often wealthy. They need to be, as hiring even a small boat for a week in June will easily set you back €2,000. The restaurants and cafés, gift shops and supermarkets that run the length of the canal would struggle without them.

We soon found that we had mixed feelings about the rental boats. There were just too many of them, which wasn't the fault of the holiday makers, but a consequence of the number of boats permitted to use the waterway by the relevant regulatory body. Moorings quickly became full, there were long queues at locks, and it felt like we had started out on a quiet back-road which had suddenly turned into the M25 on a Bank Holiday Monday.

Chapter 14

Le Canal des Deux Mers

For over 200 years the banks of the Canal du Midi have been lined by thousands of plane trees, their lofty canopy as integral to the scenery here as the canal itself. In 2006 they began to die back, infected by an incurable canker, a microscopic fungi that spreads through the root system. The disease proved to be unstoppable. Twelve years later almost all of the original 42,000 trees have been systematically felled.

We met many boaters who knew the canal before this happened, and all of them mourned the loss of these beautiful trees, saying it just wasn't the same without them. The hard reality of it is that if you've never seen something, it is hard to miss it, and so we could only judge it on how it was now, rather than how it had been. As we cruised by we could see that the banks had been replanted with thousands of disease-resistant young trees – pine, poplar and oak – with trunks barely thicker than my finger. It was almost as if the plane trees had never been, but then we would come upon an area where the final stage of the clean-up operation was still going on.

We watched as heavy-duty machines grubbed out the last bit of each tree, a solid stub of trunk with a girth that those young replacement saplings could only dream about. The machines ripped the trunk from the soil, exposing a dense network of roots beneath it, tendrils reaching out blindly as if still looking for a safe place in which to take root and grow. Finally it was dragged along the canal to a collection point and burnt.

As we saw the size of what was left of these fallen giants, smouldering charcoal-black in their mass graves, we couldn't help but understand that something majestic had passed away. It will be many years before the new saplings, so spindly and fragile, are established to the same level, but the Midi has already seen a number of massed replantings of trees in its history and will continue to do so – nothing lasts forever.

If the banks were denuded of trees, the wild flowers were doing their best to fill the gaps. We spent our days cruising through a never-ending garden, drifts of scarlet poppies interlaced with pale lilac scabious, daisies, wild geraniums, and so many other plants not known to me. I kept meaning to look up their names but never did. It was enough just to enjoy them, and to spend a peaceful half an hour during the evening picking a posy for the dining table.

In mid-May the weather had a nervous breakdown and returned to winter. We woke to temperatures of six degrees centigrade, but with the wind chill it felt much colder. We dug out our winter clothes for walking the dogs and lit the wood burner for warmth in the evenings. The wind gusted past us at seventy kilometres per hour and the locals looked ever more glum. We used the downtime to begin our home-brewing experiment.

During our smallholding days Michael made his own beer, from scratch, with raw ingredients of malted barley and hops. We didn't have the facilities or space to do that on the boat, but were going to experiment with a couple of shop-bought kits instead, one for beer and one for an elderflower cider. It took a day to do each of them, with the finished beer decanted into a 25-litre barrel. Twenty litres of cider was bottled up and stacked out of the way at the bow end. Now all we had to do was exercise the necessary restraint and wait two weeks before sampling them.

The colder weather lasted almost a fortnight and then

disappeared as abruptly as it had arrived. The temperature shot back up to twenty-four degrees centigrade, so the winter clothing got packed away again and shorts and t-shirts came back out, but the winds stayed with us. It seemed that they were a feature of this region, to the point where they had been given names.

The dry wind was called *le cers*, and when that subsided, *le minerve*, a humid wind, stepped into the breach. They routinely gusted 40–60 kilometres in one direction or another, and getting into locks and moorings can be tricky if a strong side wind is blowing you where you don't want to go. The first few weeks on the Midi we would see high winds forecast and sit them out for a day or two. Eventually we realised that they were going to be there for the duration and just got through them as best as we could.

The Canal du Midi passes through the heart of two major cities, Carcassonne and Toulouse. Carcassonne is a massive tourist attraction, the second most-visited monument after the Eiffel Tower, and there are two ways to experience it. The first is to join the thronging crowds crawling all over it, becoming one of three million tourists visiting each year. We weren't entirely convinced about this, given our aversion to busy places, but it seemed crazy to be moored up so close and not visit.

The French have an imaginative, sometimes quirky, approach to art and this year, from May to September, Carcassonne had been chosen as the backdrop for a piece of artwork that flummoxed most people and enraged quite a few others.

It had been commissioned to celebrate the anniversary of twenty years as a Unesco World Heritage Site, and was designed by a contemporary Swiss artist called Felice Varini who specialised in putting large-scale graphics on iconic buildings. This particular work was entitled 'Concentric, eccentric' and consisted of thin strips of aluminium painted a lurid, fluorescent yellow, arranged in concentric circles which were then plastered across the vast expanse of Carcassonne's gigantic buttresses and fifty-two towers.

'What is the point of that?' said Michael.

'No idea.' I cocked my head to one side and took a step back.

'Need to ask Felice Varini.'

'Since when did huge yellow circles of sticky tape count as art?' He snorted in disgust. 'It's just bad graffiti.'

Varini himself was apparently delighted with the effect, but the local people tended to agree with Michael, describing it as 'filthy' and protesting that it was ruining their lives as they had to look at it every day. There was also a sense of outrage that such an incredible and ancient fortress, part of the national heritage, should be treated with what they saw as a lack of respect. We could only agree with them. It seemed incongruous, entirely out of place and a huge waste of money. When this was put to Felice Varini his reply was that he was used to this reaction to his work, and that, eventually, people got used to it.

The second way to see Carcassonne, and one we found preferable, was from a distance. We cycled out along the back lanes, past orderly rows of vines, for no more than a couple of kilometres, and it was like stepping back in time. Nature had provided its own artwork, a field of red poppies blowing gently in the breeze, rolling themselves out like a giant red carpet up towards the outer walls. From this vantage point we couldn't see any tourists and the view of the fortress was simply magnificent, as grand and imposing as when it was newly constructed – apart from the yellow sticky tape.

Toulouse, the second city on the Canal du Midi, seemed to us to be a very different place. As strangers passing through, stopping for only a few days, our appreciation of places is limited to what we see in that short time, but this city felt less of a tourist attraction and more real, a place where people lived and worked and had families. The architecture was gracious and pleasing, with leafy squares lined with restaurants and cafés. We watched people stopping at tables to greet each other and got a sense of a strong, friendly community.

The other good thing about Toulouse was that the hire boats didn't come this far. Peace was restored.

From here we joined the second of the canals that made up the Canal des Deux Mers, the Canal de Garonne. We had gained the impression from speaking to other boaters that this canal was much quieter, possibly even a little boring, but we found it to be delightful and preferred it to the Canal du Midi.

Without the big tourist attractions we found pleasure in the smaller things: a trip down a side-arm of the canal to Montauban which coincided with their annual canal fête; the beautiful abbey in Moissac; the magic of the music festival in Agen on the summer solstice. We had our moments of adventure as well, running aground on the River Baïse, which runs close to the canal and is navigable for fifty-seven kilometres. It was in full spate and unnavigable on our way down, but by the time we returned the water had subsided. Unfortunately it was now being used for irrigation on the surrounding farmland, which in turn meant that the depth was prone to wild fluctuations and could catch you out – as indeed it did.

We almost ground completely to a halt on the way down to Montauban, trapped in weeds so thick that Olivia's propeller jammed solid. The only way to free it was to go into reverse, spitting the weeds out in the process, and then going forward a few more yards before repeating the exercise.

Best of all though was the overwhelming sense of peace, so strong I could feel it coursing through my veins, of idyllic, remote mooring spots which we had all to ourselves; of carefree days cycling into the hills, exploring hidden lakes and *beaux villages*; of fields full of sunflowers under endless blue skies; of getting up late and going to bed late, spending the long summer nights sitting on deck waiting for the stars to come out. I had a moment of sadness when we finally reached the end of the canal at Castets-en-Dorthe, a sense of a very special phase of our journey coming to an end.

But that feeling didn't last for long. From here we had to retrace our steps back the way we had come, all the way back along the Midi, braving the hire boats once more, up the Rhône and then into central France. Once we'd done that we would be on new ground once again, and who knew what we would find?

Chapter 15

Relationships

I sat at the table in the galley, put my hands over my ears, and counted to ten.

It didn't help. Nothing blocks out the whine of an angle grinder hard at work. Michael had decided today was the day to attack the peeling paintwork on the steps up to the top deck. In his armoury was an impressive array of hammers, chisels and various electrical attachments all designed to screech and scratch away until there was barely any paint left on the boat at all.

I had decided today was a writing day. My novel had wandered up yet another dead end and if I couldn't get it back on track soon there was a good chance that the whole lot would end up in the canal. Our respective tasks for the day were hardly compatible, but eventually silence fell. I breathed out a sigh of relief and turned my attention back to page 156.

Tap, tap, tap. Tap, tap, tap.

Now it was the turn of the hammer and chisel, reverberating equally through the hull and my head.

'Is it too much to ask for a bit of peace and quiet once in a while?' I yelled up at the roof above me.

Tap, tap, tap.

'Right, that does it.' I slammed the lid of the laptop shut and stormed outside, treading on Maddie's tail as she scuttled belatedly out of my way.

'I'm going for a bloody walk.' I glared furiously at Michael's back.

'Really?' He turned round in surprise. 'I thought you wanted to write today. I came up here to get out of your way.'

My mouth opened but no words came out. This would have been the point at which to turn on my heel and slam the door behind me, but there was no door to slam. Instead I just stomped off. I didn't need to look behind me to know that he would be gazing after me with a bemused expression on his face.

Ten minutes later the peace of the canal had worked its usual magic and my bad temper melted away. As I walked I pondered on relationships and what makes them work.

Living in a small space, twenty-four hours a day, every day, is a test of any relationship. If anybody reading this is considering buying a boat for long-term travelling, I would recommend you stand back and take an objective look at how you and your partner interact before signing on the dotted line.

Michael and I spent about ten seconds considering this element of our new life. This isn't quite as stupid as it sounds as we had lived, worked and spent our leisure time together very happily for the past fourteen years. We were already as good as joined at the hip and were reasonably confident that we could weather the odd fraught moment that living in the confines of a small space might throw at us. If anything, our relationship had grown stronger since we had lived on Olivia, but there were still times when the only thing to do was go for a walk and get some perspective.

I had wondered if we would be lonely in this new life, and whether making a conscious decision to isolate ourselves from friends and family might not turn out to be something we regretted. I found the reverse to be true, often in ways that surprised me.

Modern technology makes it much easier to keep in touch. We try and spend as little time as possible looking at screens, but WhatsApp proved to be a great way to share what was going on in our lives and those of our friends and family. When you are far from home, it is the minutiae of life that you miss out on, the banal, everyday things in all our lives that keep relationships strong and in the moment. A simple thought, a funny snapshot, or even a gripe about the weather, all can be shared so easily now, regardless of distance.

More importantly, the very fact that our friends and family were now so far away made me appreciate how precious these relationships were. When people are on the doorstep, it is easy to take them for granted. Now, a trip back home to catch up with everyone feels as if every moment is quality time. Since leaving the UK, I am closer to many of my friends and family members than when I lived in close proximity to them and I never expected that to happen.

The sense of being part of a community whilst we were on the boat was also a source of unexpected pleasure. Boating people look out for each other, and being a stranger or speaking a different language is no barrier. If you are ever in trouble, they will always stop to help, offering advice or spare parts with great generosity of spirit which, in turn, becomes self-replicating. The spirit of do as you would be done by must float in the ether around boats; it's never mentioned but it's always there. With a problem solved, it seems the natural way of things to celebrate by sharing a drink together. In fact, most encounters either begin, or end, with sharing a drink.

On land, I've always found it takes time for an acquaintance to become a close friend, but on the water that timeline seems to move into a different mode. It helps that we all share a common bond – a shared interest in boats and travelling, a shared appreciation of how life can be lived. It is also a relatively small community, and with only so many canals to travel upon, paths will cross over the years. There is always plenty to talk about, for many fellow boaters have lived unconventional lives and have tales to tell.

Some of these chance encounters may never move beyond a passing acquaintance, but others deepen over time and become lifelong friendships. For all of us, I think there is an instinctive understanding that our nomadic lifestyle casts a different light on relationships. If there is a sense of connection it should be grasped with both hands. Come the morning we will have moved on, and that moment of connection may not come again.

We were learning that our social life had an ebb and flow about it. We could cruise for a couple of weeks with conversations being limited to polite passing of the day with lock-keepers or passers-by, and then a boat would pull up next to us one night and we could find ourselves sitting out on deck with a bunch of raucous Italians, drinking liqueurs and philosophising until the early hours.

After a few days on the Midi we came across a couple from Wales, travelling on a catamaran who went by the name of Doris. Doris might sound like she was of a rather staid nature but her owners, Sarah and Si, had saved up and taken two years out from work for an incredible adventure down the Danube, across the Black Sea, through the Bosphorus, around the Greek Islands, along the Italian coast and into southern France. This just goes to show you can never judge a boat by its name.

When we met them they were on the home stretch, heading for Bordeaux, and we shared the journey up the Canal du Midi and along the Garonne with them, leapfrogging each other as we went. For all four of us, the journey was the richer for sharing it, for turning a corner and seeing a friendly face, and spending the evening comparing how our days had been.

Somewhere in my musings I had turned around and headed back towards Olivia. I could hear the rhythmic, staccato tap of Michael still working hard on deck. My last thought as I walked towards him was that there was one central element in all these relationships, and that was me. For a moment I managed to stand outside myself and I could see yet again how this life on Olivia was changing me.

Apart from my relationship with Michael, there had always been a part of me that stood back from getting too deeply involved with people. Deep down inside, where perhaps only I would notice it, something had shifted. I could see more clearly that to embrace relationships, rather than standing back, makes life far richer for everyone.

Michael lifted his head as I approached and I waved at him.

Now it was time to go and apologise for my temper tantrum, although with any luck, and on past experience, he wouldn't have actually registered that there had been anything to apologise for.

Chapter 16

The art of joie de vivre

It was a warm sunny day in late June and Michael and I were sitting on a wall, our bikes beside us, eating a picnic lunch after a steep pull up to the small hilltop village of Auvillar in the Tarn-et-Garonne. With its striking circular corn exchange and ancient timber-framed arcade houses, this hamlet was one of the *beaux villages* of France, a title that gave it official recognition as being exceptionally beautiful. We had visited quite a few of these villages in our travels before we had Olivia. Some lived up to expectations, others didn't seem particularly different to anywhere else, but Auvillar proved to be worth the long trek up the hill.

I watched a group of men setting out long trestle tables and chairs on a flat grassy area on the other side of the road. A poster pinned to one of the trees advertised a communal village meal and a disco taking place here tonight.

'Do you think the French enjoy life more than we do?' I asked.

'Do you mean us personally, or British people generally?' Michael took a long swig of water and sighed in appreciation.

'Both, probably. When we have a picnic we throw a

sandwich and a couple of biscuits in a rucksack and eat it in ten minutes. If they have a picnic they set it all out beautifully and take two hours over it.'

'That's because they talk more than we do. They say the same thing over and over.'

'I think it's because they're more convivial than we are. They like to do things together. And they make an effort to do it properly. Like this.' I pointed at the tables, which were now being transformed by an efficient team of the local ladies, shaking out colourful tablecloths over the dull, bare wood and placing vases of flowers along each table.

'And they go out cycling in groups. And walking in groups. Think how many times we've seen them out on a Sunday morning along the towpath, all chatting away, waving at us, making jokes. They seem really happy.'

'It wouldn't make me happy. All that chatter would just ruin a good walk. Each to their own though.' He put the water bottle back in the pannier and hopped onto his bike. 'Time to go. You ready?'

'You see? That proves my point exactly. We've only sat down for ten minutes and ...' He'd gone. I sighed and gave up.

As we coasted back down the hill, I pondered on whether the concept of the French *joie de vivre* and the stereotypical image of us Brits as being reserved and slightly inhibited by comparison was real or imagined. I suspect the truth is somewhere in the middle and that different countries have fun in different ways. I am sure the great British reserve is becoming less of a national trait with each new generation, but in my heart I feel the French still have the edge on us.

The summer solstice on June 21st illustrated this point very well, for it is a national festival day in France. We were making our return trip back along the Garonne and happened to be in Agen on that day. With no real idea what to expect I set off for an after-dinner stroll around the town and found myself in the musical equivalent of the Tower of Babel.

A local, amateur kettle-drum group were vying with a folk group, a rock band were drowning out a ladies' choir, and a disco and a karaoke were holding their own against each other but not managing to keep much of an audience. I wandered through the town and found music on every corner, down every side street. Some was terrible, some was wonderful, but it didn't matter either way for it seemed as if the whole town had turned out to see them, all dressed in their finery and enjoying every minute of it.

In Lyon, on our way back up the Rhône, we moored up right in the heart of the city. Walking along the quayside in the evening, we found a local jive group had decided the weather was too good to have their usual weekly session indoors and had migrated out onto the wide walkways by the river. The unselfconscious joy on their faces as they whirled and twirled to the music in the sunshine was mirrored on the faces of the evening promenaders who had stopped to watch.

The same thing happened in the main square in Sancerre on a Sunday lunchtime, but this time it was a line dancing group, complete with Stetsons and pointy cowboy boots. I lost count of the number of back streets in villages and small towns that I walked through over these summer months, hearing the sound of laughing voices spilling out through open windows as families and friends came together around their kitchen tables, knives scraping on plates and glasses clinking.

There's no doubt that a long summer full of sunshine helps with finding that *joie de vivre* outdoors, but it seemed to me that the French find it wherever they are, that they carry it in their hearts, or as part of their DNA. This may just be a foreigner's romantic view of the French but, as I loitered in those back streets, an outsider, a stranger just passing through, I couldn't help but envy them.

Chapter 17

A bad business

'This will do us nicely.' I looked at what I could see of the little town of St Étienne and thought it seemed a pleasant and quiet spot.

We have moored up in seventy-five different moorings in four months of travelling so far this year and yet I still get a sense of quiet relief when we find a good spot for the night. Once we arrive, a set routine takes place. Mooring lines go out, two on the bow end and two from the stern, the four ropes combining to keep us from moving too much from front to back and also from twisting from side to side. We see a surprising number of boats loosely tied on with just two ropes, see-sawing wildly with the wind or wash, and perhaps we overdo it, but better safe than sorry.

The next job is to bring everything inside and store it away for the night: binoculars, VHF radio for calling the locks, knives for cutting our ropes should they ever get jammed up on a bollard (which has happened), charts and cruising guides, life jackets if we needed them in the large locks. Then, most importantly of all, the kettle goes on. Unless we've had a very long day, in which case it's a beer or a cider.

This feeling of satisfaction at the end of the day was even more keenly felt on this particular evening as we were making our way back up the Rhône and good moorings were not always easy to find.

'Come and have a look at this.' Michael was standing at the top of the ramp leading to the shore, mug of tea in hand, reading a noticeboard. I cast a quick eye over it.

'It's just the usual stuff. There's a *boulangerie*, a *mairie*, not much else by the look of it.'

'No, not that. This.' I walked up closer and now I could see a few handwritten English words, scrawled across the bottom of the board in thick black marker pen.

'Rope cutter at 2 am. DO NOT STAY HERE!'

We stood and looked at it for a minute.

'There are no other moorings for miles,' I said.

'It could just be some kid's idea of a joke.'

'Then it would be in French, not English.' I downed the last of my tea. 'Time for a visit to the *mairie*. I'll see what they have to say about it.'

I eventually found the *mairie*'s office on the far side of the town. A notice on the reception door informed me that it was closed for the afternoon. I muttered something uncharitable under my breath about nobody in France ever working a full day, but then I heard voices from a room at the other end of the hall. I walked softly up the hallway and put my ear to the door. Men's voices, several of them. I hesitated for a moment. They might not appreciate me barging in on them, but I had a brief image of Olivia cut adrift, floating blind in the darkness, and of us waking up wide-eyed and terrified. We would be easy prey for a big commercial barge or the hotel boats, caught in their lights like a rabbit in a snare. I decided I needed some answers and so, whoever these men were, they'd have to put up with me interrupting them. I knocked on the door.

It opened to show a room full of men seated around a desk. I apologised for disturbing them, explained about the writing on the noticeboard and asked them if it was safe to moor here for the night.

There was a moment's silence while they looked at me. Then

one of them got up and patted me on the shoulder as if I was not quite all there.

'*Pas de problème, Madame. Pas du tout. Ne vous inquiétez pas.*'

The door was politely shut in my face and that was that.

I returned to find that another boat had arrived and its owners were out on the quay talking to Michael. Their faces turned towards me as I walked down the pontoon.

'What did they say?'

'Nothing helpful. They just fobbed me off. Either they don't know anything about it, or they do, but they're not going to admit there's a problem.'

Between us we proffered up various suggestions to make us feel better about being there. It probably happened ages ago, maybe it was a local feud, and so on, and then we went back on board our respective boats. Later in the afternoon another two boats turned up and, as there was no space left on the pontoon, rafted up alongside us. One of our new neighbours turned out to be an English/Austrian couple making their way from Norway to Gozo in a small yacht. It is quite common to give a gift when you moor up alongside someone, a courteous thank you for offering them a safe place to stay, and these gifts are usually of an alcoholic nature. The beers were out almost before they'd tied onto us and when we'd all run out of cold beer we moved on to wine.

At some point fairly early on we did tell them that this might not be the safest mooring they'd ever been on, but by then we were all past caring. There was also a sense of safety in numbers, possibly misplaced, but it helped. We did have enough sensibility left in us by the end of the evening to dig out our mooring chain, solid, heavy-duty metal rather than rope, and secure ourselves firmly to the pontoon with it. It took some finding, eventually turning up right at the bottom of the locker, but we had purchased it for just this sort of eventuality. We had always assumed it would be used as an insurance policy against kids playing around, rather than in this more sinister situation, but it did give us some peace of mind. Unless the evil perpetrators had a pair of seriously heavy-duty bolt cutters on them, Olivia Rose should still be safely moored alongside when we woke.

Sleep came surprisingly easily and we woke in the morning to find everyone present and correct, with no more than a slight hangover to worry about. We swapped contact details with our new friends and all went our separate ways. Later that day we entered into the port of Cruas, a pleasing place despite being situated right beneath the cooling towers of a nuclear power station. The harbour master directed us to our berth and then asked us where we had come from. When I told him we had been at St Étienne I saw his face change.

It seemed there had indeed been a knife-cutting incident there, just a few days before we had arrived. It had happened to a retired couple, who had awoken to find themselves drifting in the middle of the river in the early hours of the morning. They had managed to get back in and tied up as best they could for the night, which was not easy as all their mooring lines had been slashed. I cannot imagine that they got any sleep at all in what few hours of the night were left. They scrawled the warning message that we had seen and arrived here in Cruas the next day, very shaken by the event.

'That could have been fatal. They could have hit a bridge. Or a commercial barge could have been coming down. He'd never have seen them in time …' I trailed off. This was every boater's nightmare. It didn't bear thinking about. 'Those poor people.'

The harbour master nodded. 'It's a bad business.'

'Do they know who did it?'

He shook his head. He'd supplied them with new ropes and they had carried on because there would have been nothing else to do, but I imagine the hope and belief that most of our fellow men are decent people would have been severely tested.

A bad business indeed.

Chapter 18

Heatwave hell

'I think I'm dying.' I wiped a clammy hand over my sweaty forehead. 'I've only just got out of a cold shower. How can I be this hot already?' I flopped back weakly on the bench, fervently wishing I was anywhere but here.

We were stuck in Fragnes, on the Canal du Centre. It sounds a bit like a song title but I think even the most gifted lyricist would have struggled to make a song out of the reason why we had ground to a halt here. A big barge had bashed into a lock gate further down the canal and taken it clean off its hinges. The VNF were being non-committal about how long it would take to fix, maybe three weeks, maybe less, maybe more, maybe it was just impossible to guess, and so boats all along the canal were stranded in whatever port they found themselves in, with no choice but to wait it out. It was early August 2018, peak holiday season, so that was a lot of boats.

If you've got to be stuck somewhere, Fragnes is as good a place as any. Fragnes wasn't the problem. The problem was that we were also stuck in a heatwave, with temperatures close to forty degrees centigrade, staying there day after day, and not getting much cooler at night. Boats are not good places to be in very hot weather for they are a combination of a tin can and a greenhouse, the metal of the hull and decks holding the heat in and the countless windows, which make Olivia such a light and airy space, heating the inside like a conservatory.

We have nine windows in the galley and none of them open. The only ventilation comes from a push-up hatch at the far end. The bedroom has four windows, only one of which slides open. It does have two hatches on the back which are great if the wind is in the right direction, and useless if it's not. The wheelhouse is all windows, nine of them, wall to wall sunshine, none of which open, but both doors slide open and that is our main source of air movement. If we leave the boat and have to shut these doors the temperature inside rockets to unbearable levels in minutes.

There are things we can do to mitigate the effect of the heat. All blinds and curtains are pulled shut as soon as we wake up in the morning. We have three additional reflective blinds which we move to follow the sun during the day to try and deflect the most intense heat. We have one fan which works when we have shore power and another that works on the batteries when we are off-grid. But the heat still gets in and Olivia hangs on to it. It builds very quickly and thirty to thirty-five degrees centigrade becomes the normal temperature on board, which is why you sweat as soon as you do so much as lift a little finger.

Cooking inside was a complete no-no. We bought a camping stove and gas cylinder and cooked up on top deck. We tried sleeping out there too, but the deck slopes away on either side, something we'd hardly noticed when walking about, but which became very noticeable once we tried to lie down on it.

On top deck, where we usually sit, we have a 'bimini', a sun shade built specifically to fit Olivia, which keeps the heat off when cruising and sitting outside. It has no sides, deliberately, as we don't like to be shut in, but the downside is that it gives us no protection once the sun moves from its midday zenith. To keep it out we have sheets we clip onto the bimini and we can move these around as we need to. We soak them with water. We soak the deck with water. We never walk anywhere with bare feet as every bit of metal becomes scalding hot. I feel exhausted just writing this down – imagine how it feels to be constantly moving things and dowsing everything down in almost forty degrees of heat. Plus that's the temperature in the shade and not on a hot boat! The heat had become our enemy and it wasn't a battle we could ever win.

Mooring places with nearby trees which offered shade were like gold dust. Boat owners would scuttle off their vessels, place their chairs possessively down under a tree, no matter how small it was, no matter how thin the leaf cover, and defend these tiny spaces to the hilt. We all became experts at learning how the sun moved through the sky during the day, inching our chairs around every hour to get the maximum relief.

When it all got too much to take, we would get the water hoses off the boat and hose ourselves down, standing either in swimwear or fully clothed on the quayside, soaking ourselves in blissfully cold water, from head to toe. I always preferred to have shorts and t-shirt on as they kept you cool for longer if they were drenched through. Never before or since has a shower under a hose felt so good. The slightly orgasmic sighs that wafted along the quay would have been amusing if we weren't all so very uncomfortable.

The dogs suffered too. Their walks became so short as to be non-existent. Lucy has a really thick coat even in summer and we were continually brushing her to try and reduce it. We showered them with water and kept them in the shade. Maddie found herself a little spot right inside the centre of a hedge near the boat, the only clue that she was there being her lead trailing out and the sound of her panting. She had the best of it – I'd have crawled in there with her if there had been room.

I thought it might just have been us Brits who were suffering, as we're not used to twenty-five degrees never mind forty, but the French and other Europeans around us were as fed up with it as we were. The human body isn't built to function in temperatures like these. It wasn't a normal year anywhere on the planet. There were horrendous wild fires raging from Sweden to Athens, droughts beating all records worldwide, and floods in Japan with millions of people being told to evacuate their homes. Even in the UK, temperatures were in the mid-thirties and farmers were having to feed their animals with the hay that was supposed to be their winter feed as there was no grass for them. I couldn't pick up a newspaper or browse the internet without words like 'unprecedented' and 'catastrophic' leaping out at me, and for the first time the term 'hothouse Earth' came into being.

We all told ourselves that this was a very unusual year and next year would be better. It's just as well we can't see into the future. And yet if we could, just this once, it might scare us enough to start doing something about it before it's too late.

In the end we could bear the heat no longer. Michael took the train and picked up our work/camper van from where it was stored back in Châlons-en-Champagne. We packed it up and headed off to the Jura mountains in search of cooler air, squeezing ourselves into the last available space in a campsite almost exclusively taken over by the Dutch. We found a lake and sat in it for three days.

For a dog who is scared of pretty much everything in life, Maddie has no fear of the water. In this heat, she adored being in the lake and we struggled to make her come out at all. Every now and then we would pull her back to shore, thinking after twenty minutes paddling round endlessly in circles that she might be tired, or terminally dizzy to the point she couldn't stop, but all we got was a growl and a curling lip and she would be back in the water as soon as our backs were turned.

Lucy, so bold and fearless for most of her life, simply wouldn't go in further than wetting her paws, and that only with much coaxing. Because her eyesight was getting worse, she also got very distressed if we tied her up and left her to go swimming. We were only a few yards away but she couldn't see us and, with her hearing also very diminished, she couldn't hear us either. We took it in turns to go swimming so that one of us was close to her. Each evening saw us returning to the campsite looking like the proverbial wrinkled prunes, but it was worth it.

In the end, the VNF managed to fix the gate within the week and so we were all on our way. A huge thunderstorm cleared the air and temperatures dropped for a few days so we could all breathe again. Unfortunately it was short-lived. Before long the temperatures were soaring and we spent all our time hiding from a cruel sun. I thought back to those late spring and early summer days when the sun was gentle, and then forward to the autumn when the air turns crisp and the morning mist dances upon the water. High summer, when it's as brutal as this, comes in a poor third.

Chapter 19

The end of summer

When holidays used to last no more than two weeks there was always a point, usually a day or two before the end of the holiday, when thoughts of everyday life at home would start to intrude. Those unwanted thoughts were a persistent, irritating niggle that took the edge off those last few precious days.

It seems that the same process happens when the time away has expanded to six months, with some default setting in my brain taking a perverse pleasure in telling me that our idyllic summer was as good as over. We had made the firm commitment not to spend another winter on the boat, returning instead to the UK to earn some money, which in turn would allow us to come back out again for another summer season without hugely depleting our savings.

It was early September, so we had at least a month left, but thoughts of a long winter back in the UK began to prey on my mind and I felt as if I was in limbo, adrift between the past and the future. It was unsettling, the more so because this year, for the first time in my life, I had no home to return to. There was literally nowhere for me to lay my head.

Part of me was excited, ready for a change and looking

forward to seeing family and friends again. The other part of me was slightly anxious. If we wanted to keep this lifestyle going for many years to come, we needed to find a way to earn enough money over each winter interlude to sustain it. There was no room for failure because the thought of going back to our old life was simply unthinkable.

While we spent those last precious weeks working out how to manage the next six months as landlubbers once more, Olivia pulled out all the stops to keep us in France. It was as if she knew we were deserting her and had enlisted the natural elements to try and change our mind.

'You need to get out of bed,' said Michael. We were moored up in a beautiful spot at the Écluse de la Gazonne on the Canal de Briare in central France, quiet and peaceful, and all by ourselves.

'Why?' I cradled my mug mutinously in my hands and slipped further beneath the duvet. 'I thought we were staying here another night. What's the hurry?'

'There's something you need to see.' He threw my shorts and a t-shirt at me and pulled the mug out of my hands. 'Trust me. It'll be worth it.'

Muttering indignantly I pulled on my clothes and went up on deck.

'Over here.' Michael's voice came from the other side of a line of trees.

I pushed through the undergrowth in what I hoped was the right direction. Michael was standing with his back to me, looking out on a lake. The trees on the bank formed a perfect arch around him and if I'd been an artist I would have been rushing for my sketch pad. I went and stood next to him, ruining the symmetry of the moment, and then I saw why it had been necessary for me to get out of bed.

I'd seen so many misty mornings, but none like this one. This mist was a living thing, endlessly circling and turning in upon itself, clinging to the water like a lover who knows their time together is short. I could feel no wind on my face but all over the lake the mist was being pulled reluctantly skyward, delicate wisps of white candyfloss that became ever more transparent until, suddenly, there was nothing left and the water was quite alone and perfectly still, reflecting the trees and the hint of blue from an early morning sky in a perfect mirror image. I felt as if I had stumbled upon something mystical, timeless, and in that moment I could understand why early mankind had seen gods and spirits in the natural world all around them.

I got up early the next morning in the hope of seeing it again but, whilst the mist still hovered over the water, something was missing. The wonders of this world are fleeting. We catch them when we can, but it is a mistake to expect them to come again.

Our last few days were spent on the River Yonne. Although this is a sizeable river, it doesn't take much commercial trade, and so it felt very different to the Rhône. Leaning out over the rail as we chugged along, I could see another world in the crystal-clear water flowing slowly below me, with hundreds of tiny fish darting through tresses of green fronds. A kingfisher landed briefly on the rail at Olivia's bow. I didn't realise it was there until it flew off, a flash of blue in the corner of my eye.

The contrast to the canals was marked, for their shallow waters are often murky, even more so as passing boats stir up the mud from the bottom. Where a river runs, the canal is a static thing, the water only moving when the locks empty and fill, or when the wind gusts across it.

Before we had Olivia I considered canals to be dead bits of water, and would always choose to walk beside a river rather than a muddy ditch. Now I've spent so much time on these muddy ditches I have come to love and value them, but there's nothing quite like the thrill of peering down through clear waters and seeing so much life in them. It brings back memories of being a child again, when everything was strange and wondrous.

The locks on the Yonne were big ones but they weren't deep, so there wasn't that enclosed, coffin-like feel to them and it added to the pleasure of the experience. Unusually for a river, these locks closed for lunch, and we soon found that this caused mooring issues.

'We're going to arrive at the next lock on the dot of midday I reckon.' I scanned the charts. 'Doesn't look like there are any mooring points anywhere before it.'

'No worries. We'll moor up at the lock itself.'

All locks had their own mooring points, necessary if you were waiting for a boat to come through from the other direction and, of course, if you hit the lunchtime, down-tools slot.

All locks except this one.

'Where's the logic in that?' demanded Michael.

This was annoying because it meant we would have to use the engine to keep us steady, every few minutes reversing back against the current. It was entirely doable, but it was tedious and a waste of fuel.

'We'll put the anchor down,' said Michael. 'Might as well check it works.'

This was another new experience for me. It's common practice on seagoing vessels, and Michael had often bemoaned the fact that we had never done it. The reason we hadn't was because of the dogs. Anchoring off meant you spent the night with no way to get ashore, not such a good idea with doggy ablutions to take into account. We did hear a tale of someone who had trained his dog to stick its bottom over the side of the boat when required, but had decided this was a salty sea-dog tale and not to be taken seriously. This would be a short stop, and as I had no intention of hoisting Maddie's back end over the side, the dogs would have to cross their legs.

'What happens if there's nothing for the anchor to grab onto?' I leant over the rail, watching the chain clunk out of its housing and disappear below into the weeds. 'Wouldn't a strong current drag us along the river bed?'

'It's not so much the anchor as the weight of the chain that keeps us in place. There we are – she's out.' Michael turned the engine off. 'Time for lunch.'

This was the first time we had moored up without being tethered to the land and I was surprised at what a difference it made. It was as if we had become part of the river, no different to the weeds and stones, just something else of no consequence for it to flow past. The current moved us gently from side to side, more so than when firmly tied to a bollard on the shore, giving the impression that we were adrift, even though I knew we weren't for the anchor, or the chain, was definitely doing its job.

Being on the water like this without the engine chuntering away was also a treat. It's not a particularly noisy engine, but it's always there. People who say that you can't hear silence may be scientifically correct, but not everything in this world can be explained by statistics. I sat in the sun with my slice of cheese, a little blob of chutney and some fresh bread, and I listened to the silence.

It was perfect.

Despite all this, it was time to leave France and Olivia, just for a while. There is more to being content than beguiling waterways and blue skies. Deep inside me I felt a need to see my homeland again. I had never really appreciated that there are two distinct elements to that word, but then I had never been away from my own country for so long before. The 'home' element conjured up pictures of faces familiar and dear to me, people who speak my language, where the customs and ways of doing things are second nature and feel natural, like breathing.

The 'land' is just as important though, and I had a real yearning to set my feet on footpaths both new and well known, to feel the British wind, rain and sun on my face, to run my eyes over the contours of a landscape that was mine. My land. I didn't own it but it was still mine and I had to go back. I needed to know it was still there, top up my memories and connection to it, and then I would be ready to leave again come spring next year.

Olivia would be spending the coming months in a different situation to what she was used to. The boatyard we had chosen was on the River Yonne, which regularly flooded in the winter, and so she would be coming out of the water, lifted up by a crane and settled down on chocks in the boat equivalent of a car park. Another reason for choosing this particular location was that she needed a new prop shaft, which can only be done on land, and we wanted to paint the hull when we came back in the spring.

It's only when a boat comes out of the water that you realise how much is below the waterline. Olivia looked huge, hanging in the cradle of the crane above our heads, and that image was reinforced when she was finally in place and we had to climb ten feet up a ladder to get in the door. There was no way the dogs could get up there, so the van became their new kennel for a few days, while we cleaned and scrubbed and made her shipshape before leaving her.

'Have you looked inside this oven?' said Michael.

'I do my best not to,' I replied, as I scrubbed away viciously at the kitchen sink, wondering why we always feel it necessary to clean a place when we are about to leave it and won't get any benefit from all that effort.

'It's disgusting.'

'That's why I don't look at it. Close the door and pretend you didn't see it.'

'What happened to all those womanly instincts that make you want things sparkling and clean?'

'I haven't got any.'

Michael sighed, pulled on a pair of Marigolds, and hunkered down on his knees in front of the oven. I walked over and kissed the top of his head.

'I should hire you out. You'd make a wonderful cleaning lady.'

Our mood became increasingly sombre as the day wore on, and not just because cleaning was a chore. We were going back to the UK for all the right reasons but it suddenly hit us that it was all over for the year. We were leaving the magical part of our lives and heading back to a more humdrum existence.

I compiled the material facts of the last six months. We began the season in early March with temperatures of minus ten degrees centigrade and frozen canals. By high summer we were wilting under a relentless sun and enduring temperatures of around forty degrees. We had travelled 3,563 kilometres (2,227 miles), cruised along 13 canals, eight rivers, and made our way through 776 locks. Our deepest lock was on the Rhône at a depth of twenty-three metres and our longest tunnel was Le Grand Souterrain at just over five kilometres. We started in northern France, travelled down the spine of the country all the way south to the Canal du Midi, up the Canal de Garonne almost to Bordeaux, where we retraced our steps, eventually arriving at our current position on the River Yonne approximately 130 kilometres south-east of Paris.

Facts and figures, interesting as they are, provide a purely clinical summary of a journey. There is no colour, no feeling, no story being told. We would hold our own story, our own memories, in our hearts, bringing them out when the long winter evenings got too long, and we needed something to keep us going.

A memory surfaced of a recent conversation with a stranger. He had a home in Spain and another in the UK, both of which he loved. He'd told us that he was never completely happy in either, that he always wanted to be in the one he was not.

I could easily see how that might happen to us this winter, that it might feel that we were just killing time until we could return to Olivia. I hoped that wouldn't be the case.

Chapter 20

Learning to be landlubbers

I don't like caravans. They are white, plastic, cumbersome, all look the same and have no character about them. In our life before Olivia we had campervans and motorhomes, old ones with personalities and an overwhelming urge to deplete our bank accounts. They were money pits, perpetually either recovering from one breakdown or working themselves up to the next, but this didn't stop us travelling all round the UK and Europe and loving it.

Given my strong feelings about caravans no-one is more surprised than I am to find myself living in one. I hardly dare admit that I even quite like it. Or at least I do when I'm inside it. From the outside it is still a plastic box on wheels, just like the one on a pitch nearby, and the only way I know it's mine is because I have two window boxes of bright yellow chrysanthemums outside our door. For those who know, or care, about such things this particular box is a Swift Challenger, eleven years old, and we have bought it for the price of £6,000, which feels like money well spent considering that a new one will set you back around £20,000.

It is 5.4 metres long by 2.4 metres wide, which equates to

about half the length of Olivia and roughly a metre less in width. The interior is in immaculate condition, with shower, kitchen, permanent double bed and separate sitting/dining area, a good heating system, a light and airy feel to it and a large, sturdy awning that is perfect for coats, boots and muddy dogs.

This was going to be our home whilst we were back in the UK. We had made the conscious decision not to tie ourselves into a rental property as both the rents and the agency fees seemed exorbitant, and most landlords don't want dogs. This caravan would be our own space, to do with as we wanted, and it gave us the freedom and flexibility to stay in one place or to move on as we wished. We had considered buying a motorhome, but it would have cost a great deal more than the caravan and it would mean we had to pack everything away every time we went to the shops or to work and that wasn't appealing. I thought of this caravan as a land-based version of Olivia, but I couldn't imagine that I would ever give it a name or have anything like the same feelings for it.

We had decided to base ourselves somewhere new, in Shropshire, rather than returning to Wales. After seventeen years in what the Welsh describe as God's own country, it was time for a change and we had always found the Shropshire hills appealing. We struck lucky in finding ourselves a farm campsite for a good rate and bedded in for the winter.

Our goal was simple. We aimed to earn enough to cover all our living costs for the time we were in the UK. If we only had to dip into our savings pot for the months we were living on Olivia that pot would last much longer, giving us a good number of years cruising without leaving us totally depleted at the end of it, whenever that might be. We would never have enough money to buy a house again, at least not in the UK, but that was the choice we made when we decided to do this.

There had been moments in the few weeks before we arrived back in the UK that I experienced a sense of quiet panic. With no home to go to we would, in a way, be homeless people. As soon as we bought the caravan, those feelings disappeared and I realised I didn't have to own a house to have somewhere that I could still call home. Our society conditions us all to think that bricks and mortar are the only way to go, but there are other options, and I imagine that these will come more to the forefront now that the next generation has such an uphill struggle to get on the housing ladder.

Our income would come from three sources. We still had the equipment from our carpet and upholstery cleaning business, which was how we used to earn our living before we sold up, so it would be a relatively simple thing to launch this anew on the unsuspecting residents of Shrewsbury and surrounding villages. Our second income stream would come from a completely different route. I am a qualified Pilates teacher and intended to offer classes in the local village halls. Lastly, I have a diploma from the London School of Journalism, with a decent portfolio of travel articles and features published over the last few years, so I was looking forward to running some writing classes as well.

Our first few weeks were spent leaflet dropping and cold calling on hotels, restaurants, pubs and B&Bs for carpet cleaning, with different leaflets for the Pilates and writing classes. We advertised in local parish magazines, in shop windows and post offices, online through forums and hubs, and I made sure that everyone who came to any of my classes knew that they would get a special rate for carpet cleaning if they wanted to take advantage of it.

We have restarted our various businesses every time we've moved house and so are used to this routine. The difference this time is that we would only be here for six months. Bringing in enough of an income to make it a worthwhile exercise in such a short time would be a stiff challenge. I've always felt that we might be experimenting like this for a while, fine-tuning the process each winter, but I was sure we would eventually get something workable. All things are possible if you keep at them.

In the end, we found ourselves doing five different jobs. The farm where our campsite was based had diversified into fishing lakes and had plans to plant new hedgerows and trees around the site. Before we moved into carpet cleaning, we had run our own garden design and landscaping business and so, not surprisingly, our farmer was more than happy to employ Michael to plant these up over the winter.

The last finger in our pie was one of those strange coincidences that could never have been predicted. I answered an advert for a small company wanting a 'Girl Friday' to help out part time in their craft hobby-cum-small-business. They ended up with a 'Man Friday' as well, with Michael sanding down templates, and me cutting and sticking the components together for something known as a 'beading tray', which is a device for storing beads, used by people who make jewellery from beads as a craft hobby. Many of these trays were sent over to America where beading is big business. Apparently, wealthy American women will pay thousands of dollars to go on luxury 'beading' cruises, with lectures, demonstrations and work sessions. Proof yet again, if it were needed, that there's 'nowt so queer as folk'.

All of these five jobs were part time and flexible so we could work them in around each other. We often worked weekends as well and, between the five jobs, we did indeed manage to be self-supporting for those winter months. It felt like a real achievement, each week buying us more time on Olivia, and we enjoyed the variety. The only difficulty was knowing which hat to wear when answering phone enquiries. In the end, it was easier to answer by our own names, and then try to work out whether they wanted their carpets cleaned, their trees planted, a Pilates or writing class or an extra day sticking and cutting up at the craft barn.

It was two am and Michael was shaking me awake. I wasn't impressed.

'What are you doing? Stop it!' I elbowed him in the ribs.

'Ow. What did you do that for?'

'Because you were shaking me.'

'I never touched you! I was asleep.'

'What's that noise?'

It built slowly, like a train getting closer, a deep, throaty rumble building up to a deafening roar as the wind burst out of the trees around us, gushing and rushing past our tiny, fragile home as if it were an invisible river and we were no more than a pebble in its path. The caravan rocked wildly from side to side and I realised that this was what had woken me.

Without the solid brick or stone walls of a house to protect us against the elements we became acutely aware of the winter weather. We had experienced this on Olivia and it was happening again in the caravan. It seemed that the wind was to become a controlling element in our lives, both on the water and on land. The caravan itself was a very lightweight affair, rocking about with even a hint of wind, but it was the awning that caused us the most problems. It was a solid, heavy-duty model, tethered not just by strong pegs and storm ropes but also by being attached to the caravan itself. Strong winds would send it billowing, snapping and creaking and the caravan would rock with it. Our concern was that in very high winds it would rip and tear, leaving the contents of the awning either ruined by the rain or blown away.

Erring on the side of caution, we took our awning down twice over that winter, piling everything into the van while the rain and the wind howled around us, but thankfully that night wasn't one of those times. We settled back down and the next time the gusts came through and woke me briefly from slumber I resisted the urge to blame Michael.

If we were getting used to new routines, so were the dogs. I have no doubt that they prefer life on land rather than aboard Olivia. They've spent all their lives out in the hills and, whilst a boat gives us a sense of freedom, to them it is probably the opposite. With no water for Lucy to fall into there was certainly less drama, although she did her best to find other ways to test us.

'Where's Lucy?' I looked around anxiously. 'She was right behind me a minute ago.'

We were out for a walk in the woods with the dogs, a short drive from the campsite. We usually kept a close eye on Lucy because her sight was deteriorating rapidly but we had been chatting and our concentration had wandered. Calling for her was a wasted effort as she was so deaf. Michael whistled.

'Ouch. Did you have to do that right in my ear?'

We waited a second or two but there was still no sign of her. She'd always been a dog you could call back to you, but now that she could only see us if we were a few feet away she would get anxious if she lost us and set off with dogged determination along whatever path she could find, assuming we would be on it somewhere. The problem was that she didn't yet know these woods well enough to be blundering about by herself.

'She has to be heading back to the car. We'll catch her up.' We set off at a brisk walk, expecting to see her within a minute or two. The walk turned into a fast, panicky jog as there was still no sight of her, but at last we caught up with her. She didn't even hear us thundering up behind her and we had to get in front of her to actually make her stop.

'Considering she's nearly blind, ancient and arthritic she can't half get a shuffle on when she wants to.' I was puffing as I clipped her lead back on.

Her arthritis was getting worse. New medication had made a huge difference, but her hips were still very weak and we had to support her back end so she could get up into the van. I was dreading taking her back to Olivia: the boat itself was full of steps, while some of the places we moored were extremely challenging. It wouldn't be so bad if she would just let us lift her bodily in and out of places but she hated it so much and wriggled so furiously that it made it more difficult for both us and her. She needed to see out her last days with a big, secure garden where she could wander about to her heart's content, and I felt guilty as our new lifestyle didn't allow for that. We would just have to make the best of it. At least she had the winters on dry land.

One of the things I really missed about the UK while we were in France was a British tea room, not just because of the food, but also because they had a real emotional connection for me. The French excel at pavement cafés, concocting *patisseries* that seem to be works of art rather than something you might like to eat, but nothing beats a cosy tea room in the depths of winter.

I had just settled myself in quiet contentment in what had become a favourite haunt of mine one afternoon with a book, a cup of tea and a piece of home-made cake when some familiar faces walked in. They were new acquaintances rather than close friends, but it was nice to see them and they joined me. As was usual in this type of situation the conversation turned to what was going on in our lives.

'What do you do with yourselves though?' asked one woman.

'What do you mean?'

'When you're on the boat. What do you do with all that time?'

'Well ... we're not *doing* anything specifically. We're just on the boat.' As the words came awkwardly out of my mouth I felt they weren't a satisfactory answer and from the confusion on her face I could see she felt the same way. The question had caught me off guard and it was difficult to answer because we didn't actually 'do' anything on Olivia.

That was the whole point. We were just *on* her. It was a state of being rather than doing, of enjoying the journey rather than focusing on the destination. The joy of living afloat, beyond a one-week holiday, was one of those experiences that you simply couldn't fully appreciate until you'd done it for yourself. From her next question it became evident that it wouldn't suit everyone.

'Don't you get bored? I wouldn't know what to do with myself.'

Images of a day on Olivia flashed through my mind and I felt a pang of longing to be back on her.

'No, we're never bored.'

'What will you do when you come back?' Another person, another question. 'Permanently back I mean, not just for six months.'

'We've no plans to come back permanently. We'll keep doing this until we feel we don't want to do it any longer.'

'And then what?'

'I've no idea. I don't look that far ahead.'

They were looking at me as if I was some alien being.

'But you must miss your old home. Don't you feel vulnerable with nowhere to live?'

The questions were coming hard and fast now. I looked longingly at my courgette and lemon cake, untouched and so tempting on the plate.

'We still have a home. Two homes in fact. A boat and a caravan.'

'Well, I think it's fantastic,' said a different voice. 'I wish I could do it but I can't imagine leaving everything behind.'

I popped a mouthful of cake in my mouth and studied the faces around me. Their expressions ranged from a complete lack of comprehension, with a suggestion of pity, through to a wistful yearning. It showed me how far from the norm we had strayed. We had spent the last six months meeting people who were doing what we were doing, who thought like us, and understood the compulsion. Even in that short time, I had completely forgotten there was another way. If my life seemed strange to them, their lives seemed equally strange to me.

The conversation moved on, leaving me free to concentrate on my cake, and as they chatted about house extensions and book clubs, about tricky neighbours and the merits of the new coffee shop in town, I realised that somewhere in the last year I had passed the point of ever being able to return to what passed for a normal life. I genuinely had no idea how long we would be with Olivia. It could be five, ten years or forever. But if we did part ways with our boating life, there would still be no going back. We would move on in another direction, but going back to how we lived before wouldn't be part of it.

As winter moved slowly towards spring, and we began to think about our return date, we ran into the Brexit brick wall. The previously unthinkable concept of the UK crashing out of the EU without a deal was becoming more of a possibility each day. We felt that the implications for the country as a whole were disastrous but they were also very bad news for us on a personal level.

At present, EU regulations meant that as EU citizens we were able to spend six months of the year in Europe without having residential status. These rules would change if we crashed out. Under the worst-case scenario, we would only be allowed to visit for three months in any six. For example, if we came over in April, May and June, we would not be allowed back until October for another three-month stint. Water and electricity is turned off on the waterways from late October onwards so cruising becomes very difficult. The only way we could be on Olivia would be stationary in a port. We had bought her to cruise, not to be stuck in one place for months on end.

We hoped that there might be ways to extend this three-month limit but of course the first few months after a crash-out situation would be utterly chaotic and for a while no-one would know what rules applied. We had already had first-hand experience of what happens when the rules fly out the window with the dogs. The new travel regime would also apply to them but trying to make sense of all the conflicting information was a nightmare. They would need another rabies jab, even though their existing one was still in date, followed by a blood test one month later followed by a delay of three months to make sure they were completely clear. If we did nothing and just waited, we ran the risk of not being able to take the dogs back to France with us this year. We have a friend who runs a dog-sitting service in her home, rather than kennels, but the cost is high and our budget wouldn't allow for it.

The uncertainty and frustration became crippling. In the end we paid for the jab and the blood test so that at least the process was under way and kept our fingers crossed in the hope that we wouldn't need them. With the deadline of March 29th coming ever closer we watched in disbelief, despair and frustration as the farce in Westminster continued to plunge to new depths. When one of the reporters on Radio 4, obviously high on adrenalin, said how 'exciting' it all was I realised how out of touch both politicians and the press were from the effect all this indecision was having on ordinary people. I couldn't listen to the *Today* programme over my morning cup of tea any more. It ruined the day before it had begun.

By the middle of March the politicians were in a frenzy of voting for what they didn't want, with no-one steering a clear path for what they did want. The whole thing was incredibly depressing, not just because of the sense of helplessness and outrage at how broken and inept our system of governance was proving to be, but also because of a loss of national pride. The British had become a joke, a nation to be pitied. The final nail in the coffin was the amount of time and energy being wasted on this fiasco when the real issue of our time, climate change and the natural world, was being pushed onto the back-burner.

Almost at the deadline everybody panicked and the Brexit leaving date was pushed back to April 12th.

We decided we couldn't put our life on hold any longer and on April 11th we headed back to France. We had no idea how long we would be able to stay there but it was better than sitting at home waiting for the axe to fall.

PART FOUR: 2019

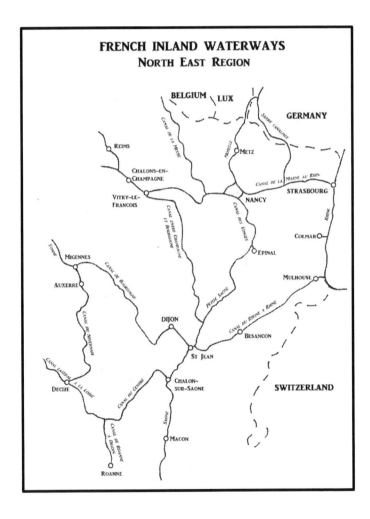

Chapter 21

Back to Olivia

'This stuff stinks.' I pushed the tin of primer out of reach, but the smell persisted.

'Wait until we start putting the anti-fouling on,' said Michael. 'That'll be even worse.'

We had been back in France for three glorious sunny days, and were now beginning the rather daunting task of painting Olivia's hull.

Our first day had been spent reorganising the inside of the boat so that it was a liveable space again. Before we had left her the previous winter all the stuff that normally sat up top – fenders and ropes, barge boards and gangways, empty plant pots, watering cans and buckets – had come down below, both for security and to make sure they didn't blow away or get damaged over winter. She was packed to the gunnels, so much so that we could barely squeeze our way through, and she reminded me of the old boats down on the Canal du Midi, full of people's furniture and junk.

Our second day had been spent sanding the hull. She was out of the river, on chocks, the decks towering above us, but the bottom of her keel was only inches off the ground. The next few days would be spent either perched awkwardly up a ladder, or half-kneeling or lying flat on the ground, roller or paintbrush in hand, straining to reach every nook and cranny.

Painting on this scale is not something any boat owner looks forward to but it has to be done to keep the hull in good condition. 'Anti-fouling' is the term for a specialist marine paint designed to prevent any type of growth, such as algae and freshwater mussels, on the hull. If left unchecked, this growth acts as a drag on the boat, slowing it down, and increasing fuel consumption.

Anti-fouling might be a specialist application but that doesn't mean there aren't a bewildering number of ways to do it and a plethora of products to achieve the required result. I had endured far too many conversations over the winter about whether we should pick a self-polishing or a non-wearing product and was now just itching to get the stuff on and get out on the water. The primer and the anti-fouling are highly toxic, both for the person applying it and the environment. If there was a truly eco-friendly version, we hadn't been able to find it.

It didn't help that we weren't the only ones donning boiler suits, goggles, gloves and face masks. Every day saw yet another boat owner arriving for the season and rolling up their sleeves. The yard was filled with the sound of grinders and sanders, occasionally broken up by the insistent beeping of the forklift truck or the roar of the crane as yet another boat was lifted into the water and sent gently on its way. The air reeked of toxins from primers and paints, from resins and varnishes and, as if that wasn't enough, the boatyard was surrounded by busy roads as well as a mainline rail station, so we could add diesel fumes to the list.

A factory opposite us spent the day spewing out a horrible smell that we couldn't begin to identify, vying with the unmistakeable stench of a sewage farm on the other side of the road. It all added up to a foul cocktail of pollution and noise on a grand scale, a full-on assault on all the senses. When my back or neck, or any other part of me, started to complain at the position I was putting it in, I would stop, look around, and despair at what we were all doing to the planet and to ourselves. For almost all of my life I have lived in the country, breathing clean air, far removed from the excesses of heavy industry. This was a new experience and I felt very uncomfortable about the part I was playing in it.

While we waited for coats of paint to dry we chatted to other boat owners around us. The conversations tended to run along the same lines, discussing where we had been, where we were going and a sharing of any useful experiences. This would be our third season on the water, but that didn't mean we weren't still the newbies on the block. Most of the people that we met had been cruising for ten years or more and so we were soaking up information rather than doling it out.

'You'll go down the Nivernais, won't you?'

This was a common question and one for which we had a stock answer.

'We'd love to but our draft is 1.15 metres, maybe 1.2. We don't think we'll get through.'

'Of course you will.'

This was from a man two boats away. We explained that we had read all the official guides, perused endless online sites and forums and the overwhelming verdict was that a boat with a depth of anything much more than a metre was likely to run aground at some point. It might not seem like much, but a few centimetres can be critical.

'You don't want to take any notice of all that.' He dismissed the accumulated wisdom of the rest of the boating fraternity with a wave of paint-stained fingers. 'It's one of the best canals in France. If you could do only one canal, it would have to be this one.'

'You'll get here.' He fished out his chart and stabbed a finger on Clamecy. 'You'll definitely have 1.3 metres up until there, so no problem. After that, if it worries you so much, you can speak to the lock-keepers each day. If the levels are low, they'll tell you. But you will get through.' He folded his chart away with a decisive snap. 'Be mad not to try.' His parting shot was not encouraging. 'It's hardly the end of the world if you run aground, is it?'

'It would be to me,' I muttered under my breath as we watched him climbing back up his ladder to his boat. Running aground was not on my 'to do' list for this year.

Boat yards are fascinating places and while our paint job was drying in a balmy twenty-two degrees – not bad for early April – we had plenty of time to poke our noses into other people's boating business.

What stories these boats could tell! The whole spectrum of boat society was spread around us, from the humble to the ostentatious, from the purely functional to the sleekly glamorous, from the pristine to the falling apart. It soon became clear that there were more boats here in the humble and falling apart category than in any other. I had often wondered what happens to boats that nobody wants any more. Looking round this yard gave me my answer. It was a veritable graveyard of abandoned vessels and dreams, rotting timbers providing a window onto their innards, the rusting reddy-brown metal of an old wreck incongruous next to the gleaming too-bright white of a plastic gin-palace. Flapping tarpaulins on a neat little wooden cruiser next to us had let the winter weather in to wreak destruction. The boat was so far gone I couldn't imagine it could ever be reclaimed. Such a shame, such a waste.

After three days of sweating and cursing in hot boiler suits Olivia was finally ready for the water again. I kept finding myself standing back from her, arms crossed, admiring our handiwork. She looked resplendent and I felt my heart swell with pride. We'd booked ourselves a slot to be lifted into the water some time on Wednesday, a loose arrangement as this is France and we were back on the 'It'll happen when it happens' schedule.

Once in the water we needed to take her out for a test drive to make sure that the new prop shaft installed over the winter was working as it should, check all the on-board systems were running, and then we would be off. I couldn't wait. If I had to breathe in any more fumes or have all my thoughts scrambled by the roar of traffic and trains and tools, I would go mad.

At last she was in. Within minutes we had water in the bilges.

You do not, under any circumstances, want water in the bilges. If the bilges fill up the boat sinks. It had been leaking in a little bit from our stern gland all last year but that had been repacked over the winter. Closer inspection revealed it was coming in from behind the stern gland, which made no sense. Then we found that the water intake for flushing the loo was also leaking into the bilges. Then the shower pump refused to play ball. Our euphoria disappeared in an instant. We did a make-do job on the water intake, and the shower pump turned out to be a loose electrical connection so was quickly fixed, but where the main leak was coming from remained a mystery.

We sucked all the water out and then gave it a good looking at. There was much head scratching from everyone concerned and the upshot was that we would wait and see what it looked like in the morning. The yard owner told us a tale of an old codger who lived on a leaky boat. He developed the habit of falling asleep with his hand hanging down by the bed. When his fingers got wet, he woke up. Not exactly a reassuring tale.

These niggling problems weren't just happening to us. Other boat owners had the same long faces as their boats were refloated. Engines didn't want to start and electrics were being temperamental. It seemed that boats don't appreciate being left.

We checked our bilges regularly over that evening and the flow of water had trickled away to almost nothing. Even so, I had an uneasy night's sleep. I tried putting my hand down over the side of the bed, my trailing fingers to be my early warning system. Needless to say they didn't stay there once I did eventually doze off, but thankfully they weren't needed and we didn't sink overnight.

Come next morning we were of the opinion that this was going to be one of those hard-to-find leaks and it was best to just get going. It was the Easter weekend and the canals would shut down on Easter Monday so we weren't cruising far, back to our mooring from last year at Laroche St Cydroine. It was only two kilometres downriver, but it was quiet and the air was fresh. I sat on deck that night and watched a perfect full moon slip out from behind the trees and float into the skies. We were home and the season had begun.

Chapter 22

The Canal du Nivernais

'Are we ready for the off?' I yawned sleepily. I'm notoriously slow to wake up in the morning and often don't have breakfast until we're under way.

'Nope,' said Michael. 'The batteries are almost flat. We have to go back to the yard.'

Suddenly I was wide awake. 'How can they be flat?'

'Something is draining them. And before you ask, I have no idea what it is.'

And so our first morning saw us back at the boatyard instead of cruising serenely along the lovely River Yonne. Simon, the yard owner, knocked us up a new battery connection, things were switched around and in two hours we were off again and thankfully, this time, we didn't come back. The electrics on Olivia needed a total overhaul at some point, but 'some point' is decided by budget and the annual repair budget had already been spent with the work carried out over the winter. It would have to wait.

We had decided to try our hand at the Canal du Nivernais. Even if we only got as far as Clamecy we would still have done roughly a third of it, which was better than doing nothing. Our first night was spent moored beneath the towering walls of Abbaye St Germain in Auxerre on the River Yonne. The restaurant Chez Max, just the other side of the path from us, was doing a roaring trade. The pavement tables were full and we sat idly on deck at our very own Chez Olivia, watching the French doing what they do best, eating and drinking, meeting and greeting, everybody keen to enjoy the warm weather. They watched us too, as our pre-dinner drinks moved on to a simple bowl of pasta, and I wondered what they made of us.

The next day the rain and the wind came in with a vengeance and Chez Max lost all its customers. We retreated indoors and lit the wood burner. Michael spent the day studying the wiring, which got less comprehensible the more he looked at it and is likely to be his life's work. I scurried around putting out bowls to catch the drips of rain coming through various leaky hatches until I ran out of bowls. Things had deteriorated over the winter. Olivia was in need of some serious TLC.

Life on board felt very different this year. We had been through hundreds of locks since we began in 2017, on rivers and canals small and large, and we were beginning to know how all the different systems worked. We had become comfortable and more competent in our roles, which meant we felt more relaxed in ourselves, and that feeling was strengthened as we found the Nivernais to be a very gentle, rural and intensely peaceful experience. Much of it was cattle country, with placid Charolais munching their way through verdant pasture land, the grass knee high and peppered with buttercups. Having spent so many years in Wales where all land is nibbled to within an inch of its life by the sheep, we've never got over the sheer novelty of seeing grass that is allowed to grow. The land gently unfurled like a giant carpet rolling up to the hills, tiny lanes hidden behind the hedgerows, and the villages and townships were old France, locked in a time warp of yesteryear. It was serenely beautiful.

It was also very quiet. Canals were built to service trade routes, and the road and rail networks that came after them often followed the same routes, which means that some waterways can be noisy. The Nivernais's trade was timber, felled from the great forests of the Morvan, floated down the River Yonne and eventually into Paris. Perhaps the rural origins of its early trade explained the lack of traffic. Whatever the reason we were grateful for it and, if we had known what awaited us later in the year, I would have mentally bottled it up and stored it to see us through.

If we luxuriated in the peace and stillness, so did the wildlife. The swallows were arriving, swooping and diving around us in the evenings. One rather raggedy and exhausted little chap landed on our guard rail for a prolonged rest, giving us ample time to study him. Grebes patrolled their patches in husband-and-wife teams. We spotted what looked like a fluffy growth on the back of one female, which turned out to be her chicks hitching a ride on her back. I wondered at what point she would decide they were strong enough to fend for themselves and eject them into the water for their first swimming lesson.

There were hardly any other boats on the canal. As always, we seemed to have started the season before everyone else. We moored up in Bailly, renowned for its wine cellars. Since wine takes precedence over food in the boating world, we felt sure we would have some company here, but we were '*touts seuls*' yet again. The mooring was free but the electricity and water were out of order. This happens all the time in France and, because you pay nothing for the mooring, it seems uncharitable to mutter about things not working. It's just how it is.

The wine cellars at Bailly were impressive, a four kilometre stretch of vast caves buried deep in the heart of the hill. They began their life as a quarry; the stone was excavated and transported for such prestigious projects as Notre Dame and the Eiffel Tower as well as the Abbaye St Germain in Auxerre. After that they became a mushroom farm and, now in their third reincarnation, they are home to six million bottles of wine from a co-operative of over forty vineyards.

'That's gone straight to my head.' I swallowed the last drops from my second flute of Crémant de Bourgogne, the local sparkling wine. We had finished our tour of the caves and were now enjoying a tasting session.

'This is the way to do business.' Michael swirled the remnants of his wine around his glass. 'Ply the customers with enough free booze and they'll buy anything.'

That philosophy certainly seemed to be working. We watched in astonishment as our fellow visitors spent hundreds of euros at a time, box after box carted off and loaded into the boots of their cars. We were on foot and, whilst we had enjoyed the wine, we felt no compulsion to break the bank with a bulk buy. We bought two bottles. The elegantly groomed woman at the till gave me a look. I wasn't entirely sure how to take it, but I gave her one back for good measure.

A couple of days later and we found ourselves standing outside the gates of a small cycle-hire business in a town called Cravant.

'We don't know these people,' said Michael. 'We can't just barge in on them.'

'We're not barging in on them. We're just going to say hello.' The English couple who lived here had met some close friends of ours last year whilst they were on a camping trip. We had never met them and it was a tenuous link, but we hadn't found anyone to chat to for days now and I needed some social contact. 'We'll pass on best wishes from Helen and Jeremy and if it turns out to be a two-minute conversation then that's fine. We'll leave them in peace and be on our way.'

They must have been ready for some socialising too because we were warmly welcomed in for a cup of tea, a tour of the house and a detailed insight into their life history. The human race loves to talk. We meet so many strangers in this nomadic life of ours and most of them have a compulsion to share their experiences of life. We don't stay strangers for long.

We also learnt an interesting fact about the rules of inheritance in France. Apparently it is not common practice to make a will, as it is in the UK. Instead your assets go automatically to your family. If you leave a house, it is shared between the offspring and this often ends in an impasse as they have to agree whether to sell it, or to keep it. The result is that it might get used a few times a year for a holiday home or, if no-one can agree or they do not have the money to maintain it, the building falls into ruin. This explains the high number of empty, obviously abandoned houses in the villages and towns across

France.

As foretold by our neighbour at the boat yard, we reached Clamecy with no difficulty. From here we would take advice each day from the lock-keepers concerning the depth issue.

The weather had turned unpredictable, a mixed bag of hot and cold, wet and dry, even a snow flurry. We left Clamecy on a sharp, frosty, sunny morning, the sort of morning where it feels good to be alive, and found the canal full of dead crows, dozens of them, floating in the water like crumpled black handkerchiefs. We were passing by a substantial industrial sawmill, the trees surrounding it home to one of the biggest rookeries we'd ever seen. The limp corpses being pushed gently aside by Olivia's bow wave had been shot, either for sport or because they had become too numerous and were regarded as a pest. The sparkle went out of the day and we pushed on through as fast as we could.

We were working our way up to the summit, a final push that included an apparently picturesque seven-lock staircase, immediately followed by another of sixteen locks and three tunnels thrown into the mix for good measure. Once you start these staircases you often have no choice but to keep going as mooring points are few and far between. Given that the entire time is spent out on deck, jumping around and throwing ropes, by choice you would do it in good weather. We did it in torrential rain and low cloud which obscured most of our views.

I'm not entirely sure why we didn't have a rest day and wait the weather out, and from the look on the faces of the French lock team who worked with us to get up to the summit, neither were they. Perhaps it's a peculiarly British trait, and we have all been conditioned from birth that you never let the weather stop you doing things. I was wet right through to the skin within half an hour and stayed that way for the whole day, but there comes a point when you don't feel it any more and it becomes a matter of personal pride that the weather will not win. Definitely a British thing.

Before we knew it we found ourselves at the end of the Nivernais and, although we had sniffed the bottom once or twice (a rather charming technical term which is another way of saying we were just touching the bottom, or a hair's breadth off it) we had not experienced any problems with water depth. We would be sad to leave this canal for it had been a delight from start to finish. It had taken us just short of three weeks to travel the length of it, a distance of 174 kilometres, giving us a daily average of 8.7 kilometres, although we hadn't been on the move every day. We had no doubt that this was a faster rate of progress than many would have done it, but we had sort of accepted that we weren't very good at staying in one spot for any length of time.

Chapter 23

Familiar faces, rapacious ducks and record breakers

It was the middle of May by now and we were heading back onto familiar territory from last year, the Canal du Centre. Somebody once said to me that the waterways are like a village and, once you've been cruising for a few years, a familiar face can be found around any corner. This proved to be very true for suddenly we found ourselves bumping into almost everyone we had met over the past two seasons. We had more evenings out over the space of a few weeks than we did during the whole of our winter back in the UK. There were new faces as well as familiar ones, impromptu drinks sessions that began in the afternoon, spilled over into communal BBQs and finally petered out at midnight. We enjoyed long lunches where folks would strum their guitars and the rest of us would stretch out on the grass and let the old ballads wash over us.

'Your life sounds like it's just one long party,' complained a close friend in the slightly miffed voice of one whose life was less party and more work orientated.

It was irritatingly true. The boating community is a small

one and believes strongly in living the good life. But you can have too much of a good thing and by the end of May we moved on and left them behind, still singing and still drinking. Our livers were screaming for an alcohol-free week. Or, at the very least, twenty-four hours.

Our surroundings were idyllic but war was being waged in the bird world around us. I thought I liked ducks – until I got to know them better.

'If I had a gun I'd shoot the bloody lot of you.' I glared furiously at four mallard drakes who were fighting over one female. She didn't stand a chance. Two of them were on top of her, both determined that they would be the one to have their wicked way with her first. As I watched helplessly, she disappeared completely under the water, resurfacing a few seconds later, spluttering and gasping for breath, only to find the next two lining up to jump on her. Eventually she managed to break free for long enough to fly away, but they all followed her.

We saw this time and time again on the waterside. There seemed to be a marked lack of females and they paid a heavy price for it. I was so upset by the spectacle that I googled it in the hope that understanding what was going on might make it less horrific. It didn't.

Ducks will pair up over the winter, nesting in March, and eggs are laid until roughly the end of July. During this time the female relies on her mate to protect her, but once the clutch is laid his role is over. He remains sexually active for a little longer in case the clutch is lost and they have to start breeding again, and this is why it all turns nasty. The male birds group together and they will fight over and forcibly mate with any female that appears unattached, chasing and pecking at her until she weakens. There is a recognised term for it, 'rape flight', described as a phase of anti-social behaviour, which seems to me to be something of an understatement. During this time they will also attack other species and even try to mate with other males. A definite case of too many hormones! Eventually the moult will begin and then things calm down again.

Most of the time the drakes seemed to leave a female with chicks unmolested, but there was one day when I saw a group of male ducks attack a female with a brood of eight chicks. They pestered her so viciously that she was forced to fly off just to survive, leaving her chicks scattered and defenceless. I never saw if they were reunited in the end, but there are times when the sheer callousness of the natural world is heartbreaking.

June 2019 turned out to be a month for breaking records. We passed through our thousandth lock since we began our travels in 2017. Ironically it turned out to be one of the most unremarkable locks of our time on the water so far, a tiny little thing about a foot deep that we hardly realised we'd gone through. Other records were not so easily ignored.

Late June saw the first of the year's heatwaves, unprecedented due to the fact that it arrived so early in the season, and also for being so fierce. Nîmes took the record, reaching forty-four degrees centigrade, but we endured our own little hell further north at thirty-eight degrees, both inside and off the boat. I only had to walk a hundred yards to the *boulangerie*, but even covering that short distance I was breathing heavily. The air felt thin and the heat was rebounding off the tarmac. We had to cycle eight kilometres to the supermarket for food and I felt ill by the time we got back. Forecasters were predicting that the rest of the summer would continue in the same vein. 'Unprecedented' had become another word for normal.

To add insult to injury I had been bitten from head to toe by some evil critter getting into the bedroom at night. We started to have conversations about how else we could spend our time over the worst six weeks of summer if this was going to be a regular occurrence. For now, however, there was no escape, so we just ploughed on through it and watched the weather forecasts with obsessive desperation.

The summer solstice on June 21st is a big day in France. Music and festivals occur in even the smallest hamlet, often lasting into the early hours, often with a band who really shouldn't give up the day job. Last year we had spent this festival day in Agen, the streets overflowing with people and music blasting from every street corner. This year, by chance rather than design, we spent it in one of the most isolated moorings we had ever encountered, deep in the Vosges forest, on the Canal des

Vosges. The contrast could not have been more marked for we were utterly alone, and all the usual man-made noises disappeared, cut off and smothered by the forest. If we had been able to fly over the area I am sure that the canal would have been no more than a spindly, pale green line wiggling its way through the jungle of trees that surrounded us.

There were no roads whatsoever along this stretch. Access was by boat or by bike and as there were no footpaths there were no walkers. It was wonderful. The sense of isolation was compounded in that there was no phone signal. No Wi-fi, no WhatsApp, no world news. We were in the dark.

I can't remember the last time I spent forty-eight hours without logging on. It made us face up to how dependent we had become on being able to share the minutiae of our day with close friends, of how we had become addicted to dipping into the BBC or the online papers to follow the chaos at home, the latest drama being the news of Theresa May's resignation. We had forgotten what it was like to not be connected. It took a bit of adjusting to, but we found that putting some distance between ourselves and the politics at home lightened our spirits and, with no-one to WhatsApp, we had more time to ourselves. It was an interesting experiment and, although I wouldn't like to be out of touch permanently, I could see the benefits of voluntarily turning the phone off every now and then.

Chapter 24

The Canal de la Marne au Rhin

July saw us heading east along the Canal de la Marne au Rhin. Our destination was Strasbourg, on the border with Germany, and the nature of the cruising changed the further east we went.

We were back in the land of the hire boats and in the high summer season they were as numerous as they had been down south on the Canal du Midi. We could immediately see why they were here in such numbers, for this was a romantic, mystical waterway, slicing through steep-sided hills. The slopes were cloaked in forests, criss-crossed with a network of footpaths, cool and enticing in the shade. Once magnificent but now crumbling castles perched high above the canal on sheer cliffs, and the moorings were rural and charming. If I had to pick a favourite canal, a very difficult thing to do as I enjoyed them all, I think this would be the one. The only slight negative came from our timing rather than anything to do with the canal itself. We were now in peak holiday season, and sharing this spectacular landscape with ten lads on a rental boat so laden down with crates of beer that you wondered how it was still afloat didn't add to the experience.

Up until this point our boating neighbours had been an

eclectic bunch from all over the world and we never knew how many different languages we would hear each day. The closer we got to the German border, the more we found that the German language dominated over all others. Whilst we met some Germans who were very friendly, there was a different atmosphere, a sense of drawing in and away. We don't speak any German which certainly didn't help and, whilst I had always thought that most Germans speak English, this turned out not to be the case. The majority of the Germans we met seemed less willing to engage and so it became a less social experience. Luckily for us, we had chanced upon some friends from 2018 who were following the same route but, without their company, I think we would have felt a little isolated on this trip.

The spectacular scenery was matched by some spectacular man-made inventions, most notably the Plan Incliné d'Arzviller, a boat lift designed to move boats from the top of the hill to the bottom, and vice versa. Imagine a gigantic bath tub at the top of a hill, big enough to take Olivia and two other boats of a similar size. Then see if you can imagine this giant tub sliding down a vertiginous slope on angled rails, thus keeping all boats and their occupants safely upright, all the way down to the bottom of the valley forty-five metres below. It has become a tourist attraction in its own right and two passenger cruisers spend the whole day taking tourists up and down, the drivers' faces blank and rather bored, while their passengers peer over the side in rapt fascination.

The Plan Incliné was built to replace seventeen locks crammed together over just four kilometres. It could take all day to get through the locks, but only four minutes in the boat lift. The original canal is still there and that too is now a site of local interest. The old towpath has become a cycle trail, one section of which diverts right through the middle of one of the locks, emptied of water specifically for the purpose. The lock-keepers' cottages were in the process of being renovated as *gîtes* and the whole area seemed to be on the cusp of a new life.

We got a real sense of nature taking over this man-made structure and claiming it as its own. The water, normally kept free of any obstruction by the hard work of the VNF, was now choked with weeds and reeds, allowing frogs, insects and birds to move in and stake their claim. There was a poignancy in seeing what happens to a canal once it is no longer used because some of the French canals are under threat of closure, a combination of high maintenance costs, low income, dwindling numbers of boats and regular summer water shortages all becoming more acute each year. We had always regarded the thought of such closures with horror, but seeing this opportunity for a second life, another phase rather than the end of it all, brought a little comfort. But only a little.

That sense of comfort didn't last for long. Friday is the day that the VNF issue their regular weekly update on closures or problems on the canal network. Water shortages were causing problems all over France and so we had made it part of our weekly routine to visit their website to keep up to date with developments.

Michael stared at the screen on the phone and scowled.

'Sim card playing up again?' I asked, not necessarily expecting an answer.

'The River Meuse is running low.'

'Oh.'

This wasn't good news. We had hoped to finish this season either in Belgium or the Netherlands and the River Meuse was an integral part of our route north. 'How bad is it?'

'Bad enough. They're updating all the time but it looks like it will be shut for the rest of the year now.'

The River Meuse was well known for running short of water in a hot summer. We knew that we had been taking a risk, leaving our journey on it until so late in the season, but we hadn't wanted to miss out on this trip to Strasbourg. Our gamble had backfired, so we needed to work out a new route for our journey north.

We pulled the maps out and looked at our options. At this time of the year any route changes had to take into account where we would overwinter Olivia. We hadn't booked anywhere yet, although not through lack of trying. We had identified several suitable marinas on our route, but could get no firm commitment from any of them until the current season was over. This was so very, very French and so very, very frustrating. If we had to find a new route then we would have to start the whole process all over again.

In the end we decided that instead of heading into Belgium we would stay in France, heading west and north, and see if we could overwinter in one of the marinas we had stayed at in our first season. We had struck up some good relationships in that time and would hope to get a more positive response from them. That would put us in a much better position to tackle the Meuse in early spring 2020, before the water levels dropped too low again.

Satisfied that we had a good Plan B, we put it out of mind and concentrated on looking forward to Strasbourg.

Chapter 25

Strasbourg

The Deux Rives Bridge in Strasbourg spans the mighty Rhine and, like much of the architecture in Strasbourg, it has been designed to make a statement. Cars are not allowed, only pedestrians and cyclists, and it is so wide that there is ample room for picnic tables at its highest point, as it arcs gracefully over the river, one foot standing in France, the other in Germany.

We cycled over it and onto German soil because such a feat of engineering demands to be used, but if not for the fact that the street names changed from *rue* to *Strasse*, we would have had no idea that we had crossed a border and were now in a different country. This area of France has been fought over by France and Germany many times over the centuries, see-sawing between the two national powers, and struggling to keep its own identity. In modern-day Europe, where borders on the ground have become invisible, people still heed the lines drawn on a map, or inside their heads. The belief in their own land, their own country is always strongest in those who have had it taken away from them.

Strasbourg is in the Alsace region of France, butting right up to the German border, but the Alsatians have their own French dialect and a strong identity of their own which is definitely not

German. Notwithstanding that, there is a very strong German presence in this corner of France. We had seen it on the canals but also in the small towns and villages along the way. We naturally greeted everyone with our usual '*Bonjour*' but so often got no more than a brusque nod in return. We might still be in France, but it didn't feel the same.

It all changed again the moment we walked into Strasbourg. It was like walking into the Tower of Babel, with languages from across the globe all mixing in with each other. We took refuge from the heat with a cold drink at a shady café, and tried to second-guess the nationality of the thronging mass of tourists passing by our table. Our criteria were random; we studied their clothes, their gestures, their style or lack of it, even whether they seemed happy or sad. We hardly ever got it right. I'm not sure if we were hopeless judges of nationality or whether we humans, like our cars, are all beginning to look the same.

Despite the fact that it caters so unashamedly to the tourists, I loved Strasbourg. Wandering through the alleyways and terraced houses of La Petite France at night was an enchanting experience. These lovely old buildings used to be home to the poorer folk, the millers, tanners and fishermen, but now they are now considered fine townhouses, an ironic statement on how values in our modern society have changed. We walked past softly lit restaurants, their tables tumbling out onto the pavements, people dining and smiling and laughing, raising glasses of crisply chilled white wine to their lips and waving their forks in the air as they talked.

As well as being a huge tourist attraction, Strasbourg is home to one of the oldest universities in France and the students were also dining, albeit more cheaply, picnicking out in the parks and alongside the canals, sprawling over each other in groups like a litter of puppies. It makes for a beguiling, animated mixture of the old and the young, the stranger passing through on holiday or business and those for whom this is home, and it gives the city a heart and a soul.

Time and time again as I travel, I find that the moments that stay clear and precious in my memory long after I have moved on are unexpected, often far away from the sites that are so popular with other travellers. With no preconception of what is to come, my reaction is spontaneous and personal. I have dropped the habit of poring over guidebooks and the internet to see what sites need to be visited as we cruise through well-known cities. Instead I simply take it as I find it. In doing so there is a risk that I might miss out on something incredible, but I usually find something that pleases me, and that is all I look for.

Old Strasbourg is a small area, easily manageable on foot, which makes it hard to miss the big tourist attractions even if you aren't consciously looking for them. The Cathédrale de Notre Dame de Strasbourg, at the heart of the old town, is one of those rare buildings that cannot be diminished by the crowds of tourists that overwhelm it from dawn to dusk. It is at its most appealing at night, and it is the lighting that works the magic, the illumination designed with a loving hand, drawing the eye softly over the incredible intricacy of the stonework of the main entrance and following the line of the spire up, up, up until it tapers away into the night sky, other-worldly and ephemeral. We came back the next day to visit the inside of the cathedral and look at it properly, but in daylight, whilst still being awe-inspiring, the magic had gone.

Strasbourg has two faces, the ancient and the modern. This is a prosperous, cosmopolitan, sophisticated city. Appearances matter and the modern architecture has to play its part. One of the most influential and impressive buildings is the European Parliament, which seats 751 diplomats from 28 countries[1], and represents the EU's five hundred million inhabitants. It is open to the public, free of charge, and I had an urge to visit it. Back in the UK, the country was waiting to hear who would replace Theresa May and I had an unsettling premonition that this might be the last time I would visit this country as an EU citizen.

I cycled in and chained my bike up on a railing along with hundreds of others. I am usually paranoid about leaving my bike, for fear of it being stolen, but there were vanloads of police in every direction so I figured this had to be one of the safest places

---

[1] There were still 28 countries in the EU at the time as the UK had not yet left.

I could ever leave it. I made my way to the security check-in, where the guard photocopied my passport and waved me through without once looking at me.

I spent the first seven years of my working life employed by international companies. There were never enough hours in the day to get everything done. I can remember rushing from one meeting to another, rushing to meet deadlines, rushing to get away before the motorway gridlocked on my journey home. As I walked around the European Parliament it felt very different. No-one rushed. They strolled. Easily recognisable by the identity badges hanging on a lanyard around their necks, they ambled from the coffee shops to one of the 1,133 offices or 18 committee rooms as if they had all the time in the world.

The place where the parliament formally sits is an amphitheatre on a huge scale. Each MEP has their own seat, numbered and reserved. The visitors' gallery is up in the gods, a circle of tiered seats looking down on the theatre below. We were marshalled in with practised efficiency by weary-looking officials, a conveyor belt of curious humanity of all ages and nationalities.

In addition to the 751 MEPs, each of whom earn around €105,000 per annum as well as expense allowances, there are administrative staff, interpreters, chauffeurs, security and police officers, cleaners and cooks. Parliament sits here once a month for four days, Monday to Thursday, and meets in Brussels six times a year for two days. The European Parliament exists to promote peace and well-being for its citizens. Whilst the sentiments are noble and give you a sense that they are working for the common good, you can't help but think that the common good would rather they stayed either in Brussels or here in Strasbourg and didn't waste all this money in having a completely unnecessary two-centre government.

As to how much is achieved in all those committee rooms, only those present will ever really know. My visit coincided with the last sitting day of the parliament and so the amphitheatre was almost empty. The last notices of the session were being tabled by the speaker, but nobody really seemed to be listening.

I came away with mixed feelings but probably shouldn't

have been surprised. All too often we hear of governments that are profligate with money raised from the masses, eager to talk and debate at great length without achieving a great deal. As I left the building, walking past a line of gleaming cars waiting to whisk those last few MEPs to the airport, their chauffeurs leaning against the so-shiny bonnets in the sunshine, I couldn't help wishing that some of these people were back with me in my corporate days, in the real world. A bit less of the strolling, and more of the rushing, might get more things done.

Chapter 26

Getting away from it all

Whilst we were waiting for our house sale to go through, one of my favourite daydreams of our future life on Olivia pictured us moored up in beautiful countryside, watching the sun set over the water. We would always be alone in this cameo, and the only sound would be the gentle evensong of the birds. As we fell asleep the owls would join in the concert, the sky would wrap a velvet blanket around us, littered with stars, and it would feel as if we were the only people in the world.

It's just as well I know that real life isn't entirely made up of flowery daydreams. We may have enjoyed the freedom of the road, or in our case the water, but we could only go where the canal went, and the Canal de la Marne au Rhin, beautiful as it was, proved to be one of the busiest stretches of water we had travelled, not least because we were there in peak holiday season.

On busy towpaths in towns, even in seemingly quieter villages, we had company. Cyclists hurtled past, singly and in groups, sporting their fancy lycra as proof that this was hardcore sport; runners were common companions, a few springing effortlessly along but most of them looking so pained that I never understood why they inflicted this torture upon themselves;

people walked with their dogs and their children, with their lovers and their grandmothers. Almost all these people would say *'Bonjour'* to us in passing because the French are a polite and convivial people, and we were happy to reply in kind. Sadly, by mid-summer, I felt as if I had used up a whole year's worth of *'Bonjours'*. I remember one lunchtime, moored up by a lock, when the French equivalent of The Ramblers' Association turned up en masse, heading our way with cries of delight. I could feel my lip curling and dashed down into the galley, afraid that my need for peace and quiet would overwhelm a courteous response. I felt completely 'peopled out', as if I was some sort of public property or local tourist attraction.

Children in particular seemed to be fascinated by boats. We were moored up just outside Strasbourg when one youngster decided to get up particularly close and personal.

'What is that little girl doing?' I paused in my lunchtime washing-up session. Michael came and peered over my shoulder and we watched in fascination as she knelt down on the quay beside the boat, pressed two pudgy little hands against the window, and peered in at us. We peered back in a less than friendly fashion which deterred her not one bit.

'If she gets her face any closer to that window she's going to squash her nose all over it ... oh and there she goes. Marvellous.'

She stayed like that for a while, her face distorted and pug-nosed against the glass, although I could hear her parents shouting at her to come along with them. Eventually a pair of adult hands came into view, reached around her waist and dragged her away, kicking and screaming as she went. She left behind a fine imprint of her nostrils on our window.

Other children would suddenly appear on deck with us, their exhausted parents sitting back on a nearby picnic bench with a sigh of relief at the thought of a few moments' respite from the endless questions of the very young. The bigger lads, out for an afternoon of jumping off the bridge into the canal, or smoking and playing their version of music very loudly on that same picnic bench, would cheekily ask if they could use our boat as a diving platform and, if not, could they have a Coca-Cola.

Our dogs also brought us a great deal of attention. Passing dog lovers would see Maddie waggling enthusiastically at them and that would be that. She'd be off and away down the gangplank, and they would spend half an hour petting her, asking all about her and suggesting politely but very seriously that she could do with a good brushing.

Children wanted to take the dogs for a walk or a swim. One little boy, again in Strasbourg, where they must breed a particular type of child, took great delight in throwing sticks into the water for Maddie, mostly in the path of oncoming boats.

It wasn't just the dogs and Olivia, we also were a tourist attraction. Our boat is bedecked with flowers, herbs and vegetables. It is clearly a home, rather than a boat for a few weeks' cruising in the summer, and many, many people would stop and admire the flowers and want to know where we had come from, where we were going, what we thought about Brexit or the weather. Even eating lunch or dinner was a shared experience. Meals are to be savoured and no self-respecting French person would ever dream of interrupting this sacred daily ritual, but it would be churlish of them not to wish us '*Bon appétit*' in passing and equally churlish of us not to reply in kind with a '*Merci*' and '*Bonne soirée*', although this is not an easy thing to do with a mouthful of food. I feel bad having a grump about this as it is a French custom I truly love, but you can have too much of a good thing.

There was no point in letting these frustrations get the better of us because there was nothing to be done about it, no way of escape. We were tied to the canal, wherever it led, tethered to the bank like a sacrificial goat. There were times in this busy area of France when it seemed an irony that our 'get away from it all' dream had actually brought us in closer contact with people than when we lived in an isolated cottage in the Welsh mountains.

I thought longingly of the many tranquil places we had stayed and knew that we would find times like that again, that this was just a phase and would not last forever. When we did find those moorings I promised myself I would treasure them, savouring every moment of stillness and silence, never taking them for granted.

For now, the next time that my fellow man came along I would just smile – and try not to spit out too much of my dinner as I replied to yet another '*Bon appétit!*'

Chapter 27

The final leg

In late July we left Strasbourg and retraced our steps back towards Nancy for the final leg of this year's cruising, a loop into Germany and Luxembourg, after which we would head back into France for our winter moorings. On the way we were treated to yet another heatwave. When I heard it was coming I could have cried. On 24th July 2019 Boris Johnson became our Prime Minister and that also brought me close to tears.

The small and immediate problems of our own lives tend to outweigh the bigger picture and we had other, more pressing developments demanding our attention. The unrelenting summer heat and lack of rainfall were continuing to have a devastating effect on the French canal network. In July they shut down the Ardennes Canal and the River Yonne, albeit due to lock failures rather than water shortages. We already knew the River Meuse had shut, but in August the Briare, the Loing, the Centre, the Vosges, and the Bourgogne canals all shut due to lack of water.

Every year there are closures due to water shortages but this level, six canals and two rivers, was new. Boats were being trapped all over the place. One of the online forums, WOBS (Women on Boats), set up a helpline where people stuck up north swapped their winter moorings with those marooned down south. Marinas with long-term winter bookings had no idea whether the boats would arrive and were swamped with people who couldn't get out.

It seemed that our revised route along the western arm of the Canal de la Marne au Rhin was one of the few options still open despite being short of water, but then we met a couple of German ladies with news of yet another problem. They had found the canal so choked with a massive weed infestation that their boat had struggled to get through. At times the lock gates could hardly shut or open against the thick mats of vegetation. There was a real threat that this canal too would close for the season.

Our faces fell when we heard this. So much for Plan B. The charts came out again and we concocted Plan C. One of the few areas still moving freely was the Moselle loop and so we decided we would keep going and try to find a winter home for Olivia in Germany. Whilst there are a plethora of cruising books and information on France, there is far less on Germany, so we had no idea what we would find.

The Moselle loop begins on the Canal des Houillières de la Sarre, which then reverts to the River Saar and leads onto the Moselle. We would be back on the big rivers, sharing them with the giant commercial barges, but we were used to this by now and the scenery was supposed to be beautiful.

I wish I had looked at a road map before we set off on this loop as it would have prepared me for what was to come. The rivers have cut their way through sheer hills, twisting and turning back on themselves as the contours shape their route and our man-made transport infrastructure has followed them, the whole lot funnelled through narrow valleys. At times the motorways and the major train routes followed the river so closely that we felt as if we were in a sandwich, six lanes of traffic on one side and commercial rail freight convoys forty carriages long on the other. Motorways are never silent; even in the early hours the sound is only a little muted compared to during the day. The freight trains seemed to be even more frequent at night. It was too hot to shut the windows, and on so many nights we lay awake as trains and cars thundered and roared around us.

We found brief respite in Sarreguemines, as our mooring ran alongside a pretty park and the motorway had been replaced by a major road so the noise level dropped slightly. For two nights we managed to get a reasonable night's sleep but the third night was a Friday and the youngsters of the town decided to have a group BBQ in the park, less than ten feet away from Olivia. They had as much right to be there as we did, but our patience ran thinner as the music got louder. When half-chewed chicken drumsticks started being thrown over the hedge, clattering onto the pontoon and just missing landing on the boat, it all seemed too much. Around midnight they disappeared, leaving mounds of rubbish and empty bottles scattered everywhere. Next morning, rather mysteriously, it had all gone.

We moved hastily on to Saarbrücken, but our visit here coincided with a festival weekend. Our rowdy teenagers were replaced by a rave going on until the early hours. We stayed there one night and then fled.

Another area of frustration came from the moorings. As is so often the case on the big rivers everything is large scale, set up for the commercial barges, and the pleasure boats always come second. In this part of Germany it felt as if we came way further down the scale than second and it made life difficult. Saarburg was a typical example. The mooring was a long quay with a high wall, fine for commercials, but Olivia looked like a toy boat beside it. We tucked ourselves in at one end, which is the designated spot for pleasure boaters. The only way we could get off the boat was to climb onto our roof and heft ourselves up onto the side of the quay. Getting the dogs ashore was a nightmare, Lucy squirming and panicking as the one of us on the boat tried to pass her to the other one up on the quay without dropping her. Even Maddie, who could jump anything, usually at speed, wasn't happy.

'What's that noise?' I was cleaning my teeth one night, getting ready for bed.

'Mm?' Michael was already under the covers, his head buried in his Kindle.

I turned off the tap. 'That noise. What is it?'

'Probably another train.'

'No. It's something else.' I pulled open the curtains and was blinded by a powerful floodlight. As my eyes refocused I could see a wall of steel floating past, so close that I could have touched it. It was a commercial barge coming in to moor for the night, its engines thrumming deep and strong, reverberating through the water so that we could feel it through our own hull.

'Christ, he's close.' Michael was at my shoulder, the Kindle lying forgotten on the bed.

We looked at each other nervously. We had heard tales of barge skippers mooring up as if we little boats weren't there at all, trapping the small cruisers against the quay wall until they were ready to go, even if they were there for several days.

'We should be all right. We're where we're supposed to be.'

'I know. But what about the boat in front of us?' An Australian boater had turned up earlier that evening and tied up in the middle of an empty stretch of quay ahead of us. It was never a good idea to tie up in the middle of empty quays. They didn't stay that way for long and he was right where the commercial would want to be. We watched nervously as the massive structure passed him with millimetres to spare and slotted its huge bulk neatly and very noisily right in front of his bow.

This particular commercial barge only stayed for a few hours, leaving noisily at 4.30 the next morning. We spoke to the Australian later that day but he hadn't heard it come or go. How I envied him the ability to sleep through that!

Most of the pleasure craft in Germany wouldn't dream of tying up on these moorings. They used the marinas and, after a few more disturbed nights on the commercial quays, we joined them.

'This is a very different sort of boating to France,' said Michael as we sat on deck on a Friday night in the marina at Schweich on the Moselle, watching ten men climb into a massive powerboat and head off to the river. A few minutes later we heard them roar past and were heartily glad that we were not moored up out there, for their wake would have sent us rocking like a plastic duck in a bathtub. An hour later they were back for a few drinks and by eight o'clock they had closed up the boat and gone home.

'I can't see anybody living on these boats.' I ran my eye over the ranks of white plastic hulls and powerful outboard engines strapped to the back. 'Maybe it's just a weekend thing.' Another couple of boats chugged out, waterskiers on board. 'And a speed thing.'

This marina was part of a leisure complex, with a restaurant in the middle and a large campsite the other side of it. The whole area was surrounded by motorways, running north to south, and east to west, as well as at least two major trunk roads and, of course, the ever-present railway line. Out of all the noisy places we had stayed, this was the worst. The relentless drone of traffic was bad enough in the marina, but the campsite was literally situated right underneath one of the motorway bridges.

'How can they choose to camp there? Why would anyone pay good money for that?' I looked at the rows of tents and motorhomes. The place was full to overflowing and the restaurant was doing a roaring trade. 'Is there something wrong with us that we can't stand all this noise? I thought camping for most people was all about peace and quiet and being in the nature.' ('Being in the nature' is a French phrase but we like it so we've adopted it.)

'They are in the nature.' Michael pointed to the river and the forests around. 'Somehow they must shut the noise out. It's beyond me.'

It was beyond me too but I could live with it because this was our last night. We had intended to head further north up the Moselle but we'd had enough. Further ahead we moved into Germany's industrial heartland and one look at the road map was enough to send us scuttling in the opposite direction. We weren't enjoying this. Parts of the route had indeed been scenic but not that scenic. It was time to turn back for France.

The next day saw us pass through three countries in the space of twenty-four hours. We spent the morning in Germany, the evening in Luxembourg and were in France again before I'd finished my breakfast the next day, the latter due to the fact that my skipper had woken up earlier than me, as usual, and was impatient to get going, as usual.

Luxembourg was an interesting place, from what we could see of it from the water anyway. Affluent was the word that first sprang to mind. The waterside houses were huge, many looking as if they were architect-designed at great cost. We moored up for the night in a place called Grevenmacher and, wandering around the town after dinner, found the architecture and the feel of the place quite appealing. It was also very neat and tidy, not a hair out of place.

Walking back to the boat we nodded a passing hello to an Austrian couple moored up before us and found ourselves drawn into a longer conversation by the woman.

'Do you like Europe?'

I braced myself. I knew where this was leading. 'Oh yes, very much.'

'Then why are you leaving? With the Brexit?'

She looked at us with genuine bewilderment. 'And that man with all the hair, Bo-Jo or whatever he is called, he is like a clown.'

With them speaking only a few words of English, and us speaking no German at all, it was hard to explain the complexities of the situation. I wanted to say that Brexit has divided our country and discredited our system of governance. The calibre of our leaders, historically something of which we were proud, has disintegrated to the point where they can't seem to find any of the qualities of leadership that are needed to steer us through our current crisis. The Brexit issue has paralysed us to the point where other, far more urgent matters are completely ignored. I wanted to say that many British people still believed we were stronger and better together and not to judge us all by the result of the referendum.

But I didn't have the words. It's hard enough to understand how we got to this point ourselves, let alone try to put it across in a stilted combination of French and pidgin English. We resorted to keeping it simple, agreeing that it is madness and a bad thing.

Five minutes later we were having the same conversation with the next boat along. Language was no barrier this time as they were from Luxembourg where most of the population are fluent in English, French, German, Portuguese and Italian, as well as speaking 'Luxembourgish' which is a mixture of German and French and apparently sounds like Dutch.

'So what do you think of this Brexit business?' It was the man who took the lead this time and he had a gently mocking glint in his eye as he spoke to us. 'It is a shame. I have worked in Nato for years and have a lot of time for the Brits. You know how to do things well. Or you did. In the past you have been impulsive and jumped off a cliff and it has worked out ok in the end. This time...' he shrugged and looked mournful. 'This time I am not so sure it will end well for you. Europe is too integrated, like a puzzle all joined together, and you can't just break off one bit.'

They were all very nice about it but it felt like running the gauntlet. We hadn't met anybody who had been antagonistic yet, which had surprised us, but I'm glad we don't have too many conversations like this. It feels uncomfortable having to defend your own country in this way and not something I ever thought I would have to do. Brexit reflects badly on all of us, no matter how passionately we may disagree with it.

Chapter 28

Out of the blue

I came up on deck with our mid-morning coffee to find Michael staring behind him with a preoccupied look on his face and Olivia heading for the shore.

'I think you're supposed to be looking forward. Or were you intending to crash into the bank?'

'We've just passed an entrance to a marina.' He spun the wheel sharply back on course with one hand and took his mug with the other.

'So?'

'I've got no record of a marina on the charts. Or on the DBA cruising notes.'

'Perhaps it's new.'

'Probably. It looked really nice from what little I could see.'

'We've only just got going. It's a bit too soon to stop for the night, isn't it?'

'I wasn't thinking about tonight. More about whether it might be any good for a winter mooring. I'm half tempted to go back and have a look. Or we could have a look online later.'

We supped our coffee in silence for a minute.

'Let's go back,' I said. 'What have we got to lose?'

We turned around and ten minutes later we were tied up to the visitors' pontoon. Flags flying at the entrance proclaimed we had arrived at 'Nautic-Ham'. It wasn't a huge marina but everything was new. Wide, sturdy walkways led to pontoons which faced out onto a small lagoon framed by a copse of trees. A pair of swans with two almost-grown cygnets floated serenely up at one end, a soft, clean white against the greenery.

I listened.

All I could hear was birdsong.

No cars. No trains.

The *capitainerie* was a short walk away, across an expanse of green lawns, housed in an ultra-modern square block of a building which was also home to the showers and toilets. To the left, back out on the river bank, was a massive domed structure with leanings towards the space age, but which turned out to be home to the sailing club, and to the right was a campsite. Plant borders lined the walkways but the trees and shrubs were young, reinforcing our initial impression that this was indeed a new development. Whoever owned it had spent a fortune.

'Welcome!' beamed the *capitaine* in excellent English. 'My name is Jerôme, how long would you like to stay for? A night, a week, a year?' He beckoned to a woman sitting at her computer in the lounge. 'Jan, come here and talk to your fellow English friends and tell them how nice it is here.'

'I don't need to,' she said. 'They'll soon see for themselves.'

And she was right. When you are looking for a home, whether it's a house or a boat, you know within seconds when you have found the right one. The same thing happens with moorings, which for us are homes in a way, albeit on a short-term basis. We weren't going to be living aboard for this coming winter but wherever we chose it still needed to feel right, a safe place to leave Olivia.

'We'll book in for a night, please. Maybe two.' We had learnt the hard way that you can never judge a place until you've spent the night there.

'No problem. We can sort out the payment later. Shall I give you the rates for our winter stays as well?'

Michael and I looked at each other.

Jerôme smiled. 'I think I will. You have plenty of time to think about it.'

Two days later we were in Jerôme's office signing the paperwork for our winter moorings. We had seen that he ran the place as if it was his own, very hands on, and we felt comfortable that Olivia would be well looked after over the winter. Not that we were ready to leave her yet. It was mid-August and we couldn't face the thought of going back this early. After the noise and upheaval of the past month, this little marina felt like a retreat, and we wanted to enjoy it. There were still plenty of outstanding jobs to be done on board, painting and mending various bits that were falling apart, and a whole new area to explore.

It was only when we actually stopped that I realised how badly I needed to be still for a while, to be in one place for more than twenty-four or forty-eight hours, and to be at ease there. I worked out that over this past season, we had spent on average five days out of every seven on the move. Those days when we stayed still were invariably days when we had a food shop or other chores to do. In our defence, many of our cruising days were short, so we would have an afternoon for exploring, and some places we wouldn't have wanted to stay for more than one night anyway, but even so I felt that we had got the balance wrong somewhere. Moving relentlessly on day after day had become a habit, an automatic reflex of get up, cast off, cruise and then repeat. Doing things mindlessly, on autopilot, was part of the life we had left behind. It had no place with us now.

I recalled a conversation with some old hands who had been cruising for fifteen years. When they found out how far we had travelled already in our first two seasons, they smiled. 'We were like that in the first years. Why wouldn't you be? There's so much to see. But you slow down eventually.'

We were indeed beginning to realise that we needed to slow down but it didn't come naturally. Being a full-time traveller is a very different thing from going away for a few weeks' annual holiday, where you either cram in as much as you can or spend the entire time lying sunny side up on a beach. There was an art to managing all this time that we now had, and we definitely hadn't mastered it yet. I was beginning to suspect that it might take a lifetime to get it right.

I made a fervent pledge to myself that next year we would slow down, to pretend that Olivia was a holiday cottage for the odd week, a static creature instead of fluid, and give ourselves time to get beneath the skin of the places we stopped in. But that was next year. I put it out of mind and luxuriated in the time that we had now.

I woke up in the morning with no need to do the engine checks or get ready for casting off. No need to work out how far we were going or where we might stop that night. Instead I got to know my little patch. I found blackberries and windfall apples for Michael to make into a wonderful crumble (yes, he can cook as well as drive the boat and no, he's not available).

The lady in the *boulangerie* recognised me after a few visits and began to say more than hello and goodbye. I revelled in the forgotten joy of going back to places for a second time, or meandering along the trail by the river, not just once, but every night as we walked the dogs after supper, watching the sky turn red as the sun set, the river catching the reflection and throwing it back, whilst the bats swooped and skydived around us.

I had always thought that freedom was inextricably linked to travelling, about moving on all the time, feasting on an ever-changing vista. I still think that holds largely true for me, but now I could see that it was more complex than I had first, rather naively, thought all those months ago when we began this new life. There is a freedom in stopping, slowing down, taking time to savour what is around you, rolling it around on your tongue and letting the flavours explode. I was still learning what freedom really means, learning to appreciate its many guises.

By the beginning of September Olivia's decks had been painted so white that it hurt your eyes in the midday sun, a host of small, niggling DIY jobs had all been done, my need to stay in one place for a while had been sated and, if we'd had anywhere to go, we would both have been very happy to get back on the water for another month. However, with all the closures, that wasn't an option, and so the issue of what we were going to do when we went back to the UK started to creep into our conversations.

'Do we want to go back to Shrewsbury and repeat what we did last winter?'

'From a financial point of view, possibly. We did manage to make ends meet there.' I sighed. I hate money. Whilst on Olivia I never really thought about it, beyond making sure we stayed strictly on budget each month. The money was there and we had given ourselves permission to take this time out. As soon as we go back to the UK all the old insecurities about whether we can make ends meet, whether we can earn enough to allow us to come back to Olivia next year, all bubble up to the surface and nibble away at my peace of mind.

'But we both felt lonely, didn't we?' I looked at Michael and he nodded in agreement. 'It takes ages to make new friends, proper friends rather than just people to say hello to, and if we're constantly going back and forth every six months it will take even longer. It wouldn't be so bad in summer but in winter, with those long nights and grey days, having friends around really matters.'

'How about we go back to where our friends are then, back to where we used to live in Wales?'

I thought about this. I've never been one for going back, but if anywhere had ever really felt like home to me it had been our cottage in the Brecon Beacons and a large part of that was due to the good friends we had there.

'Suppose we go back and it isn't as good as we remember it? Or it's just too familiar, even for a few months, and we get itchy feet all over again?'

'We won't know until we try,' said Michael. 'If it doesn't work out this winter, we'll think again for the following year.'

The other issue to consider was how we would earn our living whilst we were back. Managing five jobs last year had been exhausting and we wanted to organise ourselves better this time. We decided we would focus on our carpet cleaning business and put all our efforts into making that work, rather than spreading ourselves so thinly across so many different fronts. Abergavenny, our nearest town, had morphed into a much bigger place whilst we had been away, with sprawling new housing estates all around it, and Cardiff was easily reached. If we put in the legwork we should be able to drum up enough business to earn what we needed.

The first thing was to find a suitable campsite and we knew from previous experience that this would be a hard slog, hours spent on the internet trying to find the right place. Many close for the winter. Most of those that stay open charge on the basis that most of their customers are short term, a week or a weekend, which is understandable as that is exactly what most of them are. The cost ranges from £15 to £25 per night. Multiply that up to a month and it comes to between £450 to £750, which is crazy money for a patch of grass. It was also way outside our shoestring budget.

'They're all putting their prices up.' We had been sat at the computer for hours now and were losing the will to live. 'Last time we stayed at this one for a weekend it was £17 a night. Now it's £20.'

'That's £600 a month. We could rent a house for that.'

We both made a face. We didn't want to rent. The caravan suited us better.

The more time we spent looking, the more we found the same story. Camping is big business in the UK now and prices were creeping up everywhere. Many sites were investing in fancy loo and shower blocks to give themselves an edge over the competition and the result was higher prices. To the non-camping fraternity, it might seem strange that people would chose a site for its facilities over its views or location, but there's none so strange as folk, and we had all too regularly overheard campers extolling the virtues of five-star standard loos, in Europe as well as in the UK. We always used our own facilities in the caravan so we couldn't care less but that didn't help us much.

We were looking for an alternative arrangement to the norm, something called the winter seasonal pitch, a totally different beast and one that seemed on the verge of extinction as there were so few around. The situation was further complicated by the fact that a proportion of campsites that did offer this structure only offered it on the basis that, whilst you had paid up front for six months, you were not allowed to use the caravan permanently in that period.

Again, this may sound mad to the non-camper, and it sounds equally mad to us, but it has always been this way and you have to work to the rules. But after many years of camping we could clearly see how the market was changing, and none of these developments were working in our favour. We were living outside of the normal, outside the conventional bricks and mortar life and, whilst you would hope this might make life simpler, in many ways it does not.

Finally we found a site. Communication wasn't their strong point, and it took many emails and telephone calls before we could even get an answer, but the location was right and the price, whilst a little higher than we had paid last year, was within our budget.

So, we had a plan. It was time to book our crossing back and to get Olivia ready for the winter. Water systems had to be drained down and batteries sorted out. We hoped we had solved our persistent leak in the bilges. It had certainly been dry for a good length of time but it was the sort of thing that would wait until we were literally about to leave and then start to play up.

Since April we had travelled just over 1,500 kilometres, and added another 479 locks to our tally. We had passed through three countries along four canals and three rivers. We had met old friends and made new ones, learnt a bit more about what we liked and what we didn't. It had been another good year and it felt as though we were settling into this life, that it was who we were, and I was already looking forward to coming back in spring.

But I was equally happy to be leaving. I need the contrast of our two lives to be able to enjoy them both. It feels to me as if I live in two paintings, one blue and one green. The blue one is our life on Olivia. It is the colour of her hull, of the water and the sky, of a kingfisher as it flits along the tree line. The green one is our winter life, the mountains and the fields, the trees before they take on their autumn mantle and in the spring when it all bursts into life again and we leave it to head back to Olivia.

Finally, after so many years of searching, I have found a way of living that makes sense to me, one that gives me a sense of freedom, of balance, and of being in the right place. Is freedom all it's cracked up to be? It's both more and less. There are good times and bad, times of insecurity and frustration as well as of a soaring joy and deep contentment. Freedom is finely nuanced, always changing, and I think once it has a hold of you it won't let go.

Which is fine by me.

We would be going back to much uncertainty. Would our campsite arrangement work? Could we earn enough to keep going? What would Brexit do to our future plans?

Everyone has uncertainty in their lives, and we all have to work through it as best we can. The future is unknown and insecurity just another part of everyday life. One thing is for sure though. Fate must have been smiling down on us when we walked past that old barge on holiday back in 2016 and its owner asked us if we wanted to buy a boat.

If you're ever in France, or maybe the Netherlands or Belgium, maybe even Sweden, walking along a canal, keep an eye out for us. You can't miss us. Olivia is always the prettiest boat on the water, geraniums and petunias, strawberries and herbs sprawling across her decks and spilling over her gunnels. Maybe we'll have learnt to slow down, maybe we won't, but don't hang about because we'll probably be gone by the morning.

Come aboard for a drink and we can discuss the finer points of life, talk about freedom and the merits of slow living. We might even be old hands by then and, if you've just bought a boat, we can share what we've learnt and look on with amused tolerance as you boast of how many miles you've covered this season.

It might be on the tip of your tongue to ask us if that huge leap into the unknown all those years ago was worth it, but then you would look at our faces, at our lovely boat, and you would have your answer.

The End

Useful information

Introduction

This section of the book is included as a reference guide for anybody who is considering buying a boat with a view to cruising the inland waterways of Europe. I have deliberately steered away from an in-depth 'how to do it' approach. That would be another book all by itself, and that information is clearly and concisely covered in the books and online resources that I list below so there is no need for me to repeat it. The aim of this section is to point you in the right direction and back it up with advice and useful tips that we have picked up along the way.

The first half gives details of books, associations, maps, charts and useful websites. The information found in these sources will help you choose the right boat and find out where to buy it, tell you where to go and what you need to do to get the most enjoyment out of your cruising. It is by no means an exhaustive list. These are the sources that we have used and have found valuable, but you will find many others once you start looking. I also offer some advice in this section about the merits of buying a boat in the UK or in France and discuss the options for crossing the Channel if needed. All information provided was correct at the time of writing.

For the second half I have picked out my ten top tips, the ten most important pieces of advice I could give you if we were sitting down face to face, discussing the merits of life on the water. If you chatted to another boater you would most likely get another ten tips, all different, and that is a good reason to talk to as many people as possible. These suggestions are not in any order of priority, but are based on what I have learnt through personal experience.

I hope it helps and wish you many years of happy cruising.

Part 1: Sources of information

Publishers

Imray Nautical Charts and Books – www.imray.com This organisation is a useful umbrella contact for books, maps and charts.

Books, maps and charts

1. *Cruising the Inland Waterways of France and Belgium* – from The Cruising Association and edited by Margaret Harwood, Brenda Davison and Roger Edgar. We used the 2017 edition (non-member price £15) but a new 2019 version is now available, edited by Gordon Knight, £25. It provides details of all the canals and rivers in France and Belgium, as well as a useful section on equipment, legal requirements, locks, and practical hints and tips.

2. *Sell Up and Sail* (2005) by Bill and Laurel Cooper, £19.99. Useful overview of the practicalities of life afloat written by two people who have lived aboard for over thirty years.

3. *The Barge Buyer's Handbook* – The handbook of the Dutch Barge Association, £10 for members/£14.95 for non-members. Equally useful if you want to buy a motorcruiser rather than a barge, with an exhaustive list on things to look out for and advice on the actual process of buying a boat.

4. *Inland Waterways of France* (2010), £32.50 by David Edwards May. This is an old book, a cruising guide to the French inland waterways, detailing locks and moorings. Some elements are out

of date but we still found it useful.

5. Fluviacarte/Editions du Breil – these are the two options for charts, essential for cruising. They offer broadly the same information but in a slightly different format, so it is a matter of personal choice as to which you might buy. They are available by region, usually around €20 each, and are the waterways equivalent of the OS maps for walkers, albeit nowhere near as detailed.

A specific chart from Editions du Breil folds out to show the entire network at a scale of 1:1,000,000. We found this essential for forward planning. ISBN 2-913120-06-7.

Associations

1. The DBA – www.barges.org You do not need to own a barge, or even a boat, to become a member of this group. They have over 1,500 members worldwide and membership costs £40 per person including a bi-monthly magazine. They have active member forums, blogs and a website with detailed information on absolutely everything to do with cruising, from engine maintenance to an excellent mooring guide. If you join them before you buy your boat, the knowledge they will pass on will help you make the right decision.

2. The Cruising Association – www.theca.org.uk This organisation has a wider remit than the DBA, covering oceangoing boats as well as inland cruisers, with over 5,700 members worldwide. We bought their excellent book (see book section) but have not joined them as we had already joined the DBA. However, as we go further afield I am sure we will become members. Their website has over 16,000 pages of information, backed up with an app, forums and magazine. The annual cost of membership is £137 by direct debit/£148.50 by cheque or card.

Other useful websites

1. Voies Navigables de France (VNF) – www.vnf.fr/vnf The

French navigation authority responsible for maintenance of inland waterways. Provides updates of what is happening throughout the network, in French but with the option to translate to English. Certain regions have their own individual contact details e.g. www.nordest.vnf.fr for north-east France.

2. Force 4 Chandlery – www.force4.co.uk Online chandler for everything nautical – clothing, electronics, books and boat parts.

3. ASAP Supplies – www.asap-supplies.com Supplier of marine equipment, boat parts and spares.

4. The Connexion France – www.connexionfrance.com English language website all about what's going on in France. Not boat-related but gives an insight into what is happening in the country.

Boat brokers

1. H2O – www.h2ofrance.com This company is the main broker of boats in France, based at the small town of St-Jean-de-Losne. They hold twice-yearly boat sales in May and September and it is well worth a visit because it gives you the opportunity to look at a large number of boats in one location. It is an invaluable tool in helping you to decide what you do want and, just as importantly, what you don't want. For example, the larger boats give you more space, but mooring costs are higher and it can be difficult to find mooring spots big enough to take the boat. It was only when we physically stood in a Dutch barge, rather than looking at it online, that we realised it was far too big for us.

H2O are located at a crossroads of some of the best cruising in France, giving immediate access to the River Saône, the Canal de Bourgogne and the Canal du Rhône au Rhin. This offers the second benefit of allowing you to see what French canals and locks look like if you haven't come across them before.

2. Apollo Duck – www.apolloduck.co.uk There is a French offshoot as well. It runs a website that allows sellers to place an advert for boats for sale. Buyers get in touch directly with the

owner.

3. Boatshed Bourgogne – www.bourgogne.boatshed.com This operates in a similar way to Apollo Duck.

Wherever you buy your boat from, be prepared to haggle hard and look for a good discount. Should you have general maintenance or repair work carried out, be aware that costs in France are often higher than in the UK and that it is not always easy to get a fixed- price quote. Without an agreed final figure, the bill may well end up higher than you expected. This is no reason not to have work done in France, simply that forewarned is forearmed.

A note on whether to buy in the UK or in Europe

We had always intended to buy our boat in France and attended two of the boat sales at H2O with that in mind. It would have meant we could get out onto the waterways straight away, rather than have to get the boat across the Channel, but also that we would have to accept that the exchange rate was not as favourable as it had been a few years previously. We didn't find a boat that suited us at those sales. Instead we found Olivia through the Apollo Duck site and bought her direct from her owners. She was moored on the River Trent in Newark, close enough to allow numerous visits as well as a detailed handover from her very helpful owners. It is unlikely that we would have had that level of support buying from a broker abroad.

I would recommend looking both in the UK and in Europe. The most important thing is to find the right boat, regardless of where it is.

Boat haulage – crossing the Channel

If you do buy a boat in the UK, you will need to get it across the Channel. There are two options, either sailing it across or shipping it across.

This stretch of water is one of the busiest crossings in the world and the journey is not to be taken lightly. If you decide to sail a boat across, you will need to be a proficient, experienced sailor, or you will need to employ someone who can do it for you, and your boat will need to be seaworthy. Be aware also that mooring costs in ports like Ramsgate are high and soon mount up if the weather turns against you and you have to wait for a good weather window.

The second option is to ship your boat over on a trailer on a ferry. This has the advantage of being safer, quicker and is far less dependent upon the weather. It is also more expensive so you will have to decide where your priorities lie. Our priority was to get Olivia from Newark to Dunkirk as soon as possible and so we opted for the trailer. It is worth shopping around as prices vary. A good way to keep the cost down is to see if you can tie your trip in with one that the haulage company are already making, so, for example, they take your boat down, pick another one up for the return journey and everybody benefits. We used SG International Boat Haulage (www.sghaulageltd.co.uk) whom we found via the DBA Magazine. We found them to be reliable, very professional, fairly priced and good people to deal with.

Part 2: Top ten tips

1. Spend time doing your research and draw up a detailed wish-list of exactly what you want in your boat. The DBA handbook is an excellent tool to help you with this and will save you a great deal of wasted time. Think about things like engine size, air and water draft that matches the canals you want to go on, decide how much are you prepared to pay – and then add some extra cash for annual repairs, both expected and unexpected. Having done this, when you find your perfect boat the list will be completely forgotten in the joy of the moment, but it is still worth doing because it will eliminate some basic mistakes and is a great way of learning about boats.

2. Don't just look at boats online. Get inside them – see how it

would feel to have to go up and down a set of narrow stairs twenty times a day, sit in the galley and decide if it is too big or too small, picture yourself trying to fit that giant Dutch barge into a small mooring space and consider whether a smaller boat would suit you better.

3. Are you a practical DIY-type person? You'll need to be. Boats go wrong constantly, from a leaking window seal to the engine breaking down. If the most important tool in your tool box is your mobile phone for calling someone else for help, this life may not be for you.

4. Be prepared. Having the right equipment and store of spare parts is vital. It can stop a small problem from turning into a big one. Invest in a good tool kit, and put together an easily accessible box of spares: impellers, fuses, fan belt, fuel and oil filters. In times of desperation ask the boat next door. A large selection of tap and hose fittings will ensure you always have access to water. A heavy-duty chain is useful for mooring up in cities or for moorings that seem a little dodgy. Don't scrimp on a life jacket as it could save your life. Mine is self-inflating but also light and easy to wear. Buy a proper emergency medical kit and make sure you can always get at it quickly. A small, fold-away trolley will have multiple uses, from food shopping to carrying fuel cannisters, which is often the only way of obtaining diesel.

5. Try before you buy. If you have zero experience of boating this might be a good thing to consider. Hiring a boat for a week in France will give you a real insight into how it all works. Having said that, this is an expensive option and, if you do it before you've got the necessary qualifications that you will need for your own boat, you will be thrown in at the deep end and it could put you off unnecessarily. Another option is to make friends with someone who has a boat and ask them to take you out for a day. Join one of the associations, get to know people and don't be afraid to ask – we all like to help each other.

6. Learn the language. If you can learn even a few sentences of

the language of the country you are visiting, it will make a huge difference as to how you are received. This is particularly true in France, where they appreciate any effort you make, and tend to be much less welcoming to somebody who only speaks English to them. It is tempting in countries where English is widely spoken, such as the Netherlands, not to bother, but I still think a 'Hello, how are you?' in the native tongue is the best way to begin any relationship.

7. Do you want to be a full-time or part-time boater? Most people do it for the summer season, anything from three to six months. If you want to live on your boat all year round there are additional points to be aware of. Practical issues of how weatherproof it is, how good the heating systems are, financial issues of supporting yourself, legal issues of living in a foreign country for long stretches of time. The latter will no doubt be more difficult now that we are leaving the EU. You may also find that you go a bit stir crazy on a boat after a few months. This isn't unusual – take a week or two out and then hopefully you'll be happy to come back.

8. Expect some bad days and don't let that put you off. There is no doubt that this is a great life, but we all still have bad days – a scary experience in a lock, a bad mooring spot, the constant strain of not knowing how everything works or what you are doing, the boat trying to bankrupt you. Console yourself with the thought that it will make you stronger – eventually. Someone once told me that you need to give yourself two years before you judge whether this life suits you. I think we all have different time frames for feeling comfortable in what we do, but it certainly helps if you don't go in with rose-tinted spectacles.

9. Getting on with each other – you and your partner will be together all day every day, sometimes in fraught situations where it helps if you don't yell at each other when the going gets tough! It's vital that you can work together as a team, recognise that you may have different skills or roles, hopefully complementary, and to be more considerate of each other than you might need to be

when you lead more independent lives on land. With regard to relationships with other people, there may be long stretches where you don't meet many people with whom you connect. It helps if you can develop a sense of being comfortable in your own company.

10. After reading all the books, being bombarded by all this advice, feeling overwhelmed at how much more complicated the whole idea seems now you're looking at it in detail, don't give up on it. Don't be afraid to take that leap into the unknown. Every single person who has ever owned a boat will have gone through this process, so you aren't alone. I can only speak from personal experience, but I've never regretted it. Perhaps the more important question to ask yourself is not 'Do I really want to do this?' but 'How will I feel if I don't do it?' If you can't bear the thought of years of regretting not having at least tried, then you have your answer. Time to make that leap!

Acknowledgements

A big thank you to friends and family who helped me put this book together, notably Helen Isaacs for proof reading and checking my French made sense and Tricia Houlton for wading through punctuation and spelling. Michael and Antony Houlton did a great job of putting the maps together.

Publishing your first book is a steep learning curve and I am grateful to Louise Lubke Cuss at WordBlink for copy editing, Georgia Laval at Laval Editing for formatting and the team at Ebook Launch for the cover design. You were all so helpful and patient, did a great job and are now my team for all future books.

A final thank you to Michael, husband and skipper extraordinaire, who guided Olivia Rose and I through waters still and stormy and without whom none of this would have happened.

About the author

Mary-Jane is a freelance travel writer who has travelled extensively throughout Europe. Always something of a wanderer, in 2017 she and her husband Michael sold their house, bought a boat and began a nomadic adventure cruising through Europe. *Just Passing Through* is her first book, detailing their travels in France, and marks the start of a series that will follow them as they travel further through European waters.

Printed in Great Britain
by Amazon